Chinese

Business

Dictionary

Edited by
Richard Guo

Schreiber Publishing
Rockville, Maryland

Chinese Business Dictionary
Morry Sofer, Editor
Richard Guo, Chinese Editor

Published by:

Schreiber Publishing
Post Office Box 4193
Rockville, MD 20849 USA
www.schreiberpublishing.com

Library of Congress Cataloging-in-Publication Data

Chinese business dictionary / edited by Richard Guo..
    p. cm.
  ISBN 0-88400-314-0
  1. Business--Dictionaries. 2. Commerce--Doctionaries. 3. English language--Dictionarie--Chinese. I. Guo, Richard.

HF1002 .C439 2005
330'. 03--dc22

2005011050

Printed in the United States of America

Chinese Business Dictionary

Introduction

Business language around the world in the twenty-first century is in a state of rapid change. This creates the need for new business dictionaries that are not tied to the past but rather reflect the new global economy. This is particularly true in regard to an English-Chinese business dictionary, which brings together two economic systems that are far from identical. Until a few years ago, the Chinese economy was a closed socialist economy that sought to replace the Western system of free trade and capitalism. Hence, Chinese business terminology was significantly different from the business terminologies of the West. In recent years, China has transformed its economy to match those of the West, and a linguistic process was set in motion to coin new business terms. This process is still in full swing, hence the need for a fully updated dictionary.

The main corollary of this new reality is that even a new English-Russian business dictionary is not going to be exhaustive and definitive. But at least it is a start. It is to be expected that such a dictionary will be updated at least once a year or every two years at the most.

Many of the English business terms in this dictionary are very American-specific. As such, they do not always have equivalent terms in Chinese and therefore are explained in some detail.

This dictionary covers many areas of business, such as banking, insurance, real estate, export-import, stock market, and more. In addition, several hundred business-related computer and internet terms have been included.

Many of the Chinese business terms used today are directly copied from English. Some of the English business terms have both a Chinese term and an English term rendered in a Chinese form. The user of this dictionary is advised not to look upon all the Chinese terms herein included as cast in stone. Some may be questioned by business professionals in China, or in certain parts of China. But it goes without saying that the need for this kind of dictionary is urgent and it should go a long way in contributing to better trade relations between English-speaking and Chinese-speaking business partners.

Please note: This dictionary includes computer terms related to business. Such terms are followed by the indicator (c), to set them apart from the rest of the text. In some cases, an English term may have several meanings, which include computer terms. In such case, the Chinese computer term is preceded by the indicator (c).

A

abandonment
放弃、报废

abandonment clause
放弃条款

abatement
冲销、减免、注销

ABC method
ABC库存管理方法、
价值分类库存管理法

ability to pay
支付能力

abort (c)
异常终止，放弃

above the line
（资产负债表或损益表上
的）线上项目

abrogate
废除、废止

absence rate,
absenteeism
缺勤率

absentee owner
缺勤业主

absolute advantage
绝对优势、绝对利益

absolute liability
完全责任

absolute sale
完全出售

absorbed
归入、合并

absorption costing
全额成本计算

absorption rate
占有率

abstention
弃权

abstract of record
案件摘要

abstract of title
所有权摘要

abusive tax shelter
税务滥用保护条款

accelerated cost recovery
system (ACRS)
成本加速恢复系统
（ACRS）

accelerated depreciation
加速折旧

acceleration
提前偿付

acceleration clause
提前偿付条款

accelerator, accelerator
principle
加速因子，加速比

acceptance
接受，同意，承兑

acceptance sampling
验收采样

access (c)
存取，访问

- 1 -

accession
增加，取得

access right
出入权，使用权

access time
存取时间

accommodation endorser, maker or party
通融票据背书人，出票人或当事人

accommodation paper
通融票据

accord and satisfaction
债务替代清偿协议，协议与补偿

account
帐，帐户，会计科目

accountability
会计责任，经管责任，受托责任

accountancy
会计专业，会计工作

accountant
会计，会计师，会计员

accountant's opinion
查帐意见书

account executive
营业经理

accounting change
会计变更

accounting cycle
会计循环，会计周期

accounting equation
会计方程式

accounting error
会计差错

accounting method
核算方法，会计方法

accounting period
会计期间，会计结算期

accounting principles, accounting standards
会计原则，会计标准

accounting procedure
会计程序

accounting rate of return
会计收益率，投资报酬率

accounting records
会计帐册，会计记录

accounting software
会计软件

accounting system
会计制度，会计系统

account number
帐号，帐户编号

accounts payable
应付帐款

accounts payable ledger
应付款分类帐

accounts receivable
应收帐款

accounts receivable financing
应收帐款融资

accounts receivable ledger
应收帐款分类帐

accounts receivable turnover
应收款周转率

account statement
对帐单

accredited investor
受信投资人

- 2 -

accretion
自然增值

accrual method
应计方法

accrue
增值，应计

accrued interest
应计利息，
应付利息

accrued liabilities
应计负债，应付债务

accrued taxes
应计税款

accumulated depletion
累积折耗

accumulated depreciation
累积折旧

accumulated dividend
累积股息

**accumulated earnings tax
or accumulated profits**
累积收益税或累积利润

acid test ratio
酸性试验比率

acknowledgment
承认，回执

acquisition
买进，收购

acquisition cost
购置成本，取得成本

acre
英亩

acreage
英亩制土地

across the board
全面

activate (c)
激活，启动

activate a file (c)
启动文件

activate a macro (c)
启动宏(功能，指令)

active cell (c)
当前数据单元

active income
主动收入

active market
活跃市场，
流通市场

act of bankruptcy
破产法

act of god
不可抗力，天灾

actual cash value
实际现金价值

actual cost
实际成本

actual damages
实际损失

actuarial science
保险统计计算科学

actuary
理算师，精算师，
保险统计员

addendum
附约，附录

**additional first-year
depreciation (tax)**
第一年的（税务）
补提折旧

additional mark-on
额外加成

additional paid-in capital
溢缴资本

add-on interest
追加利息

adequacy of coverage
投保条款充分

adhesion contract
服从契约

adhesion insurance contract
服从保险契约

ad infinitum
无限制

ad item
附加项目

adjective law
程序法，程序规则

adjoining
毗连，贴近

adjudication
判决，宣告

adjustable life insurance
可调整人寿保险

adjustable margin (c)
可调节边际

adjustable mortgage loan (AML)
可调整抵押贷款（AML）

adjustable-rate mortgage (ARM)
利率可调抵押贷款（ARM）

adjusted basis or adjusted tax basis
调整制或税款调整制

adjusted gross income
调整后总收入

adjuster
理算人，理算师

adjusting entry
整理帐，调整分录

administer
管理，支配，执行

administered price
管制价格，受控价格

administrative expense
管理费用，行政费用

administrative law
行政法

administrative management society
行政管理学会

administrative services only (ASO)
唯行政服务（ASO）

administrator
主管，经理，行政人员

administrator's deed
管理人契约

ad valorem
从价，按价

advance
改进，提高，提前，预付，贷款

advanced funded pension plan
预收资金养老金计划

adversary
反方当事人

adverse opinion
反对意见

adverse possession
非法占有

advertising
广告，广告业，广告学

advertising appropriation
广告拨款

affective behavior
奉承行为

affidavit
宣誓书

affiliated chain
联营连锁店

affiliated company
附属公司

affiliated retailer
连锁零售商

affiliated retailer
联营零售商

affirmative action
反优先雇用行动

affirmative relief
确认赔偿

after-acquired clause
后得财产条款

after-acquired property
后得财产

after market
销售后市场，闭市后市场

after-tax basis
税后制

after-tax cash flow
税后资金流动

after-tax real rate of return
税后实际收益率

against the box
以保险箱为抵押

age discrimination
年龄歧视

agency
代理商，代理权，代理机构

agency by necessity
必需代理

agent
代理人，经纪人

agglomeration
经营集中化，企业集团

agglomeration diseconomies
集约劣势

aggregate demand
总需求，总需求量

aggregate income
收入总额，总收入

aggregate indemnity (aggregate limit)
总赔偿（总限额）

aggregate supply
总供给，总供应量

aging of accounts receivable or aging schedule
应收账款分期或定期分析表

agreement
协议书，和约

agreement of sale
销售协议

agribusiness
农工联合企业

air bill
空运单，空运提单

airfreight
空运费，空运

air rights
空运法权

aleatory contract
保险单，投机性合同

alienation
让度，转让

alien corporation
外国公司

alimony
生活费，赡养费

allegation
声明，宣告

allocate
分配，拨款

allocated benefits
已分配福利

allocation of resources
资源配置

allodial
自主拥有

allodial system
自主拥有体系

allowance
折扣，减价

allowance for depreciation
折旧提存

allowed time
放宽时间

all risk/all peril
全险，一切险

**alternate coding key
(alt key) (c)**
替用编码键（alt 键）

alternative hypothesis
替换性假设

**alternative minimum
tax**
替换最小课税

**alternative mortgage
instrument (AMI)**
可选择抵押证书
（AMI）

amass
囤积

amend
修改，订正

amended tax return
修正的税款申报书

amendment
修改，更正

amenities
舒适，适意

**American Stock Exchange
(AMEX)**
美国证券交易所（AMEX）

amortization
分期摊还，摊销

amortization schedule
摊销表

analysis
分析

**analysis of variance
(ANOVA)**
方差分析（ANOVA）

analysts
分析员

analytic process
分析过程

analytical review
分析检查

anchor tenant
主要租户

animate (c)
活动的，动画制作

annexation
兼并，并吞

annual basis
年度基准

annual debt service
按年支付债务本息

annual earnings
年收益

annualized rate
按年率计算

annual meeting
年度会议

annual mortgage constant
年度抵押贷款常数

annual percentage rate (APR)
年百分利率（APR）

annual renewable term insurance
年度可展期人寿保险

annual report
年度报告

annual wage
年度工资

annuitant
年度受益人

annuity
年金，年金保险

annuity due
到期年金

annuity factor
年金因子

annuity in advance
预付年金

annuity in arrears
拖欠年金

answer
答辩

anticipated holding period
预期持有期间

anticipatory breach
先期违约

antitrust acts
反托拉斯法案

antitrust laws
反托拉斯法

apparent authority
当然权力

appeal bond
申诉保证金

appellate court (appeals court)
受理上诉的法院（上诉法院）

applet (c)
小应用程序

application of funds
资金申请

application program (c)
应用程序

application software (c)
应用软件

application window (c)
应用程序窗口

applied economics
应用经济学

applied overhead
已分摊间接费

applied research
应用研究

apportionment
分担，分摊

appraisal
估价，评估

appraisal rights
估价权

appraise
估价，评定，鉴定

appraiser
估价师，鉴定人

appreciate
增值，赞赏

appreciation
升值，增值

appropriate
预算拨款

appropriated expenditure
拨定支出

appropriation
拨款，挪用

approved list
核准单

appurtenant
附属的

appurtenant structures
附属结构

a priori statement
外因报告

arbiter
仲裁人

arbitrage
套汇，套利

arbitrage bond
套汇债券

arbitration
仲裁

arbitrator
仲裁人，公断人

archive storage
档案保管

arm's length transaction
正常交易，公平交易

array
阵列，整列，一批

arrearage
欠款，拖欠数

arrears
欠款

articles of incorporation
公司条例，公司章程

artificial intelligence (AI)
人工智能（AI）

as is
按货样，概不保证，现状如此

asked
卖方报价

asking price
索价，要价

assemblage
组装，装配

- 8 -

assembly line
装配线，流水作业
assembly plant
装配厂
assess
估价，评估
assessed valuation
估定价值
assessment
资产评估，
税款评定
assessment of deficiency
亏损评估
assessment ratio
估价比
assessment roll
摊派税捐清册，课税清册
assessor
估算员，审查员
asset
资产
asset depreciation range (ADR)
固定资产折旧幅度
（ADR）
assign
转让
assignee
受让人，代理人
assignment
转让，分配，指定
assignment of income
收益转让
assignment of lease
转租

assignor
转让人，指定人
assimilation
融合
association
协会，公会，商会
assumption of mortgage
承担抵押贷款
asterisk (c)
星号
asynchronous
不同步
at par
按照票面价格，
按平价
at risk
担风险
attachment
查封，扣押，附件
attained age
永久保险年龄
attention
引人注意，收件人
attention line
收件人书写处
attest
作证，证明
at the close
最后价格，收市价格
at the opening
开始价格，开盘平价
attorney-at-law
律师
attorney-in-fact
代理人

attribute sampling
属性抽样，特性抽样法
attrition
磨损，消耗，减员
auction or auction sale
拍卖
audience
听众
audit
审计，查账，核数
audit program
审计计划，审计程序
audit trail
查账索引
authentication
验证，认证，鉴定
authorized shares or authorized stock
核定股份，额定股本
automatic checkoff
自动扣除
automatic (fiscal) stabilizers
自动（财政）
稳定功能
automatic merchandising
自动推销
automatic reinvestment
自动再投资
automatic withdrawal
自动提款

auditing standards
查账标准，审计规则
auditor
审计师，核数师
auditor's certificate
审计师证明书
auditor's certificate, opinion, or report
审计师证明书，意见书，或报告书
auxiliary file (c)
辅助文件
average
平均数，平均指数
average cost
平均成本
average (daily) balance
（日）平均余额
average down
低于平均价，
低于正常价
average fixed cost
平均固定成本
average tax rate
平均税率
avoirdupois
常衡
avulsion
因河水改道后土地的转移

B

baby bond
小额债券

baby boomers
婴儿潮人群

backdating
倒填日期

background
investigation
背景调查

background check
背景支票

back haul
回程

backlog
积压未交付

back office
事务部门，后勤人员

back pay
欠薪，欠付工资

backslash (c)
反斜杠，反斜线符号

backspace key (c)
退格键

back up (c)
备份

backup file (c)
备份文件

back up withholding
备用扣交

backward-bending supply
curve
向后弯曲的供给曲线

backward vertical
integration
后向垂直合并

bad debt
坏账，呆账

bad debt recovery
收回坏账

bad debt reserve
坏账准备金

bad title
失效产权

bail bond
保释保证书

bailee
委托人，受寄人

bailment
寄托，委托

bait and switch
advertising
诱销广告

bait and switch
pricing
诱销定价

balance
差额，余数，平衡

balanced mutual fund
平衡互助资金

balance of
payments
国际收支,
国际收支差额

balance of trade
贸易平衡, 贸易差额

balance sheet
资产负债表, 决算表,
平衡表

balance sheet reserve
资产负债准备

balloon payment
漂浮式付款

ballot
选票, 投票

bandwidth
带宽

bank
银行

banker's acceptance
银行承兑

bank holding company
银行持股公司

bank line
银行授信额度

bankruptcy
破产, 倒闭

bank trust
department
商业银行信托部门

bar
阻止, 律师界

bar code (c)
条形码

bar code label
条码标号

bargain and sale
无保证交易

bargain hunter
买便宜货的人

bargaining agent
谈判机构,
交易代理人

bargaining unit
谈判单位,
有独立交涉权的工会单位

barometer
晴雨表, 指标

barter
物物交换, 以货易货

base rate pay
基本时薪

base period
基准期

base rent
基本租金

base-year analysis
基年分析

basic input-output
system (BIOS) (c)
基本输入-输出系统
（BIOS）

basic limits of
liability
基本责任限额

basic module (c)
基本模块

basic operating
system (c)
基本操作系统

basis
基础, 基数, 标准

basis point
基点

batch application (c)
成批处理应用程序

batch file (c)
批处理文件

batch processing
分批加工，
成批处理

battery
殴打，电池

baud
波特

baud rate (c)
波特率

bear
卖空，空头，
负担

bearer bond
无记名债券

bear hug
熊抱式开价

bear market
熊市，淡市

bear raid
卖空浪潮

before-tax cash flow
税前现金流量

bellwether
指针性债券

below par
低于票面价值

benchmark
水准基点，基准

beneficial interest
受益权，受益人利益

beneficial owner
受益所有人

beneficiary
受益人，受款人

benefit
效益，利润，利益，
津贴

benefit-based pension plan
公司担保的养老金计划

benefits, fringe
附加利益，额外津贴

benefit principle
利益原则

bequeath
遗赠，遗产

bequest
遗产，遗物

best's rating
最佳评级

beta coefficient
贝塔系数

betterment
固定资产改良

biannual
一年两次的，半年一次的

bid and asked
喊价，要价

bid bond
投标押金

bidding up
哄抬标价

biennial
两年一次的

big board
纽约证券交易所

big-ticket items
高价商品

bilateral contact
双边合约

bilateral mistake
双边错失

bill
汇票，票据，账单，
钞票，证券

billing cycle
开单周期

bill of exchange
汇票

bill of landing
提单，提货单

binder
承保协议，暂保单

bit error rate (c)
误码率

bit map (c)
位图；位映象

black list
黑名单

black market
黑市

blank cell (c)
空白单元格

blanket contract
总合同

blanket insurance
统括保险

blanket mortgage
统括抵押

blanket recommendation
统括建议

bleed
榨取

blended rate
综合费率

blended value
平均价值

blighted area
衰落区

blind pool
委任同盟

blind trust
保密委托，盲目信托

blister packaging
发泡（塑料）包装，
薄膜包装

block
巨额证券，大宗股票

blockbuster
畅销书/影片

blockbusting
房屋唛卖生意

block policy
成组货保单

block sampling
区域采样

blowout
贱价甩卖，销售一空

blue-chip stock
蓝筹码股票，
热门股票

blue collar
蓝领，蓝领工人

blue laws
蓝法

blueprint
蓝图

blue-sky law
蓝天法,
股票发行控制法

board of directors
董事会，理事会

board of equalization
税率调查委员会

boardroom
证券交易人经纪行情室,
董事会会议室

boilerplate
标准协议，公式化语言

bona fide
真正的，真诚的

bona fide purchaser
真诚的买家

bond
债券，公债，证券,
保证金

bond broker
债券经纪人

bond discount
债券折价

bonded debt
债券负债，公债借款

bonded goods
保税货物

bond premium
债券溢价

bond rating
债券评级

book
账簿，记录，簿记

book-entry securities
记账债券

book inventory
账面盘存

bookkeeper
簿记员，账房

bookmark (c)
书签

book value
账面价值

boondoggle
无价值的事

boot
补价，附加利益,
(c) 引导程序；启动,
自举

boot record (c)
引导记录

borrowed reserve
借入准备金

borrowing power of securities
证券借入能力

bottom
底价，谷底,
最低市场价

bottom fisher
探底投资者

bottom line
净损益

Boulewarism
布里瓦主义

boycott
抵制

bracket creep
收入等级上升

brainstorming
智囊

branch office manager
分支机构经理

brand
商标，品牌

brand association
品牌联系

brand development
品牌开发

brand development index (BDI)
品牌开发指数

brand extension
品牌扩展

brand image
品牌形象

brand loyalty
品牌忠诚度

brand manager
品牌营销经理

brand name
商标名称

brand potential index (BPI)
品牌潜力指数
（BPI）

brand share
品牌市场占有率

breach
违反

breach of contract
违约，违反合同

breach of warranty
违反保证

breadwinner
养家糊口的人

break
违约，物价暴跌，倒闭，停顿

break-even analysis
保本分析，盈亏平衡分析

break-even point
损益两平点，保本点，盈亏临界点

breakup
拆售

bridge loan
过渡性贷款，临时性贷款

brightness (c)
亮度

broken lot
散批货物

broker
经纪人，掮客

brokerage
经纪业，经纪费

brokerage allowance
经纪人佣金

broker loan rate
经纪人贷款利率

browser (c)
浏览程序，浏览器

bucket shop
黑市买空卖空小交易所

budget
预算，安排

budget mortgage
预算抵押贷款

building code
建筑法律，建筑条例

building line
建筑线

building loan agreement
建筑贷款协议

building permit
建筑执照，建筑许可证

built-in stabilizer
内在稳定因素

bull
多头，买方，哄抬价格

bulletin
布告，公告

bulletin board system (BBS)
布告板系统（BBS）

bull market
牛市，好市

bunching
年度相混收入

bundle-of-rights theory
整体权利理论

burden of proof
举证责任

bureau
局，处，所

bureaucrat
官僚

burnout
透支，用尽

business
商业，企业，营业，业务

business combination
企业合并

business conditions
商业状况，行情

business cycle
经济周期

business day
营业日

business ethics
商业道德，企业道德

business etiquette
商业礼节

business interruption
营业中断

business reply card
商务回信卡

business reply envelope
商业回信信封

business reply mail
商业回复邮件

business risk eclusion
商业风险规避

business-to-business adverting
企业对企业广告宣传

buffer stock
缓冲存货

bust-up acquisition
破产并购

buy
购买

buy-and-sell aggreeement
买卖协议

buy-back agreement
回购协议

buy down
买低利率

buyer
买方，买家

buyer behavior
买方行为

buyer's market
买方市场

buy in
买进，补进

buying on margin
边际购买，
以差价购买

buy order
债券定单

buyout
买下全部股权或产权

buy-sell agreement
买卖协议

buzz words
术语，专门用语

bylaws
公司章程，细则

bypass trust
过继信托

by-product
副产品

by the book
照章办事

C

cable transfer
电汇
cache (c)
高速缓冲存储器
cadastre
地籍簿，不动产估价清单
cafeteria benefit plan
自助餐馆式福利计划
calendar year
日历年度，自然年度
call
催缴，要求偿还，买入，
收回
callable
可赎回
call feature
提前兑回条款
call option
购买选择权，
买进约定权
call premium
赎回溢价
call price
赎回价格
call report
报表，要求提供报表
cancel
取消
cancellation clause
撤消条款，解约条款

cancellation provision
clause
撤消条件条款
capacity
容量，设备能力，生产率
capital
资本，资金，股本，本金，
资方
capital account
资本账户
capital assets
资本资产，固定资产
capital budget
资本预算，基本建设预算
capital consumption
allowance
折旧费，资本消耗的补偿
capital contributed in
excess of par value
超票面值缴入资本，
溢收资本
capital expenditure
资本开支，基本建设费
capital formation
资本形成，资本积累
capital gain (loss)
资本收益（损失）
capital goods
资本货物，
固定资产

capital improvement
改进生产设备

capital intensive
资本密集型

capital investment
资本投资，基建投资

capitalism
资本主义

capitalization rate
资本化率

capitalize
资本化

capitalized value
核定资本值，资本化价值

capital lease
资本租赁

capital loss
资本损失

capital market
资本市场

capital rationing
资本配额

capital requirement
资本需求量

capital resource
资本来源

capital stock
股本，基金，股金总额

capital structure
资本结构，资本构成

capital surplus
资本盈余

capital turnover
资本周转，资本周转率

caps
上限，限额

caps lock key (c)
大写锁定键

captive finance company
控股金融公司

cargo
货物，船货，物品

cargo insurance
货物保险

carload rate
整车运费

carrier
运输行，货运商，承运人

carrier's lien
承运人留置权

carrot and stick
胡萝卜加大棒，奖赏和处分

carryback
转入以前年度

carrying charge
置存资产费用，存货囤积费用

carryover
移后扣减

cartage
货运费，搬运费

cartel
卡特尔

case-study method
案例分析法

cash
现金，现款

cash acknowledgement
现金回执

cash basis
现金交易条件,
现收现付制

cashbook
现金出纳账

cash budget
现金预算

cash buyer
现金买入方

cash cow
摇钱树

cash disbursement
现金支出

cash dicount
现金折扣

cash dividend
现金股息

cash earnings
现金收益

cash equivalence
相当现金价值

cash flow
现金流动, 现金流量

cashier
出纳员, 司库

cashier's check
本票, 银行本票

cash market
现金交易市场

cash on delivery (cod)
货到付款（COD）

cash order
现付票, 现金票据

cash payment journal
现金支出日记账

cash position
现金头寸, 现金状况

cash ratio
现金比率

cash register
现金出纳机

cash reserve
现金储备, 准备金

cash surrender value
现金解约价值,
退保金额

casual laborer
临时工

casuality insurance
意外伤亡保险

casuality loss
意外损失

catastrophe hazard
巨灾危险

catastrophe policy
巨灾医疗险

cats and dogs
可疑证券, 投机性证券

cause of action
起诉原因

CD-writer/CD-burner (c)
CD 写入器/CD 烧录机

cell definition (c)
单元格定义

cell format (c)
单元格式

censure
谴责, 批评

central bank
中央银行

central business district (CBD)
中心商业区（CBD）

central buying
集中购买

central processing unit (CPU) (c)
中央处理单元（CPU）

centralizaion
集中

central planning
集中计划策略

central tendency
集中趋势

certificate of deposit (CD)
存款单，存单

certificate of incorporation
公司注册证书，公司执照

certificate of occupancy
居住证书

certificate of title
产权证书

certificate of use
使用证书

certification
合格证，证明

certified check
保付支票

certified financial statement
已证明财务报表

certified mail
登记信（保证递送，但不保证赔偿）

C&F
成本及运费

chain of command
控制跨度，指挥系统

chain feeding
链式供应

chain store
连锁店

chairman of the board
董事长

chancery
平衡法院

change
零钱，兑换，修改，变动

change of beneficiary provision
受益人条款变更

channel of distribution
分销系统，销售网

channel of sales
销售渠道

character (c)
字符

charge
主管，要价，收费，借项，充电

charge buyer
信用购买人

chart (c)
表，图表

charter
特许，特权，租赁契约，许可证，宪章

chartist
图解专家，
证券行情分析家

chart of accounts
会计科目表

chat forum (c)
闲谈论坛

chattel
家财，动产

chattel mortgage
动产抵押

chattle paper
动产文件

check
账单，支票，核对，校正，
盘货

check digit
校验数据

check-kiting
支票骗空

check protector
支票保护器

check register
支票登记账

check stub
支票存根

chief executive officer
总裁，首席执行长

chief financial officer
财务长

chief operating officer
业务长

child and dependent care credit
儿童及家属照顾费用税务
减免额

chi-square test
交叉平方检验

chose in action
诉讼产，权利上的财产

churning
反复买卖

CIF
到岸价格

cipher
密码

circuit
电路，线路，循环，
流通

circuit board (c)
电路板

civil law
民法，大陆法

civil liability
民事责任

civil penalty
民事惩罚

claim
索赔，债权，要求，申请

class
类别，等级

class action b shares
乙类活跃股

classification
分类，分级

classified stock
分类股票

clause
条款，条例，科目，项目

clean
不附保留条件的，
清洁的

clean hands
清白，诚实
cleanup fund
后事处理基金
clear
支票兑现，结清，脱售
clearance sale
清仓拍卖
clearinghouse
票据交换所，清算机构
clear title
明晰产权
clerical error
笔误，纪录错误
clerk
职员，办事员
client
客户，顾客，买方
clipboard (c)
剪贴板
close
关闭，接近，达成，
结清
close corporation plan
股份不公开的公司计划
closed account
已结账，已结清账户
closed economy
封闭性经济
closed-end mortgage
限额型抵押
closed-end mutual
fund
封闭式共同基金
closed stock
限额股份

closely held corporation
被少数人控制的公司
close out
出清存货
closing
结束，结账，决算
closing agreement
税务结清协议
closing cost
成交价
closing date
截止日期
closing entry
结账分录
closing inventory
期末存货
closing price or closing
quote
收盘价或收盘行市
closing statement
结清报告
cloud on title
产权缺陷
cluster analysis
群组分析
cluster housing
集中建筑群
cluster sample
成群抽样样本
cluster sampling
成群抽样分析
code
代码，密码，符号，标记，
规章，标准
code of ethics
行为准则，道德准则

codicil
遗嘱更改

coding of accounts
账户代码，
科目代号

coefficient of
determination
决定系数

coinsurance
共同保险，联保

cold canvass
兜售

collapsible corporation
可随时进行清理的公司

collateral
附属，担保

colatteral assignment
间接转让，担保转让

collateralize
提供抵押

collateralized mortgage
obligation (CMO)
附属抵押品贷款义务
（CMO）

colleague
同事

collectible
可收回的

collection
收兑，收款，托收

collection ratio
收款比率

collective bargaining
集合议价，集体谈判

collusion
共谋，串通舞弊

collusive oligopoly
串通性寡头垄断

column chart/graph (c)
柱形图/柱形表

combinations
联合，合并，联合体

comfort letter
安抚信，安慰信

command
控制权，指令，支配

command economy
控制经济，中央集权经济

commencement of
coverage
保险责任开始

commercial
商业的

commercial bank
商业银行

commercial blanket bond
商业诚信保证

commercial broker
商业经纪人

commercial credit
insurance
商业信用保险

commercial forgery
policy
伪造商业保险单

commercial forms
保险单

commercial health
insurance
商业医疗保险

commercial law
商法

commercial loan
商业贷款

commercial paper
商业票据，商业文件

commercial property
商业财产

commercial property policy
商业财产保单

commingling of funds
资金混用

commission
佣金，委员会

commission broker
经纪人

commitment
承诺，保证

commitment fee
委托费

commodities futures
商品期货

commodity
商品

commodity cartel
商品卡特尔

common area
共同领域

common carrier
承运商，公共运输企业

common disaster clause or survivorship clause
共同灾难条款或生存条款

common elements
共用设施

common law
普通法

common stock
普通股

common stock equivalent
等同普通股，准普通股

common stock fund
普通股信托投资基金

common stock ratio
普通股比率

communications network
通信网络，交通网

communism
共产主义

community association
社区组织

community property
共有财产

commutation right
折偿权利

commuter
月票旅客

commuter tax
跨区工作税

co-mortgagor
共同抵押贷款人

company
公司，商行

company benefits
公司福利

company car
公司车

company union
公司工会

comparable
可比的，
可比拟的

comparable worth
可比价值

comparitive finacial
statements
比较财务报表

comparitive negligence
共同疏忽责任

comparison shopping
采购条件的比较调查

compensating balance
补偿余额

compensating error
补偿误差

compensation
补偿

compensatory stock
options
补偿性股票选购权

compensatory time
补偿时间

competent party
主管部门

competition
竞争，比赛

competitive bid
公开招标，竞标

competitive party
竞争方

competitive party method
竞争方方法

competitive strategy
竞争战略

competitor
竞争对手

compilation
编制

compiler
编译程序

compliant
应允的，服从的

complete audit
全部查账，全面审计

completed contract
method
完成合同法，全部完工法

completed operations
insurance
完工保险

completion bond
完工保证

complex capital structure
复合资本结构

complex trust
复合信托

compliance audit
依法审计

component part
构成部分，成分

composite depreciation
综合折旧

composition
和解，组成，构成

compound growth rate
复合增长率

compound interest
复利

compound journal entry
复合分录

comprehensive annual
financial report (CAFR)
综合年度财务报告
（CAFR）

comprehensive insurance
综合保险

compress (c)
压缩

comptroller
主管会计

compulsory arbitration
强制仲裁

compulsory insurance
强制保险

compulsory retirement
强制退休

computer (c)
计算机，电脑

computer-aided (c)
计算机辅助的

concealment
隐瞒，匿报

concentration banking
集中银行处理业务

concept test
概念测试

concern
公司，行号，企业，关注，难点

concession
承认，关税减让，特许，核准，让与

conciliation
调解，调停

conciliator
调停人

condemnation
征用

conditional contract
有条件合同

condition precedent
先决条件

conditional sale
有条件销售

conditional-use permit
有条件使用许可

condition subsequent
后续条件，解约文件

conference call
电话会议

confidence game
骗取信用

confidence interval
置信区间

confidence level
置信度

confidential
保密

confirmation
确认，证实，证明，批准

conflict of interest
利益冲突

conformed copy
一致的复印件

confusion
混淆，混杂

conglomerate
联合大企业

conservatism, conservative
保守主义，谨慎

consideration
互相履行义务，补偿，议，考虑

consignee
承销人，收货人，受托人

consingment
托运，寄销，交付，
委托

consignment insurance
收货人保险

consignor
委托人，托运人，发货人，
货主

consistency
一致性

console
控制面板

consolidated financial
statement
合并决算表

consolidated tax return
综合所得税报表

consolidation loan
统一贷款

consolidator
集装业者

consortium
国际财团

constant
常数

constant dollars
定值美元

constant-payment loan
定偿贷款

constituent company
分公司，子公司

constraining (limiting)
factor
限制因素

construction loan
基建贷款，工程贷款

constructive notice
推定通知

constructive receipt of
income
推定收入

consultant
顾问，咨询

consumer
消费者，顾客

consumer behavior
消费行为

consumer goods
消费品

consumerism
消费主义

consumer price index
(CPI)
消费物价指数

consumer protection
消费者保障

consumer research
消费研究

consumption function
消费函数

container ship
集装箱船

contestable clause
可抗辩条款

contingencey fund
意外开支准备金

contingency planning
应急计划

contingency table
质量管理相依表

contingent fee
应急费

contingent liability
不确定债务

contingent liability
(vicarious liability)
不确定责任
（转承责任）

continuing education
继续教育

continuity
连续性

continous audit
连续审计

continous process
流水作业

continous production
连续生产

contra-asset account
资产抵消账户

contract
合同，契约

contract carrier
契约承运人

contraction
萎缩，订约，签约

contract of indemnity
赔偿契约

contractor
承包商，签约人

contract price (tax)
合同价格

contract rate
约定费率

contract rent
约定地租

contrarian
反向投资人

contribution
捐献，贡献，分配，分担

contribution profit,
margin
边际利润贡献

contributory negligence
共同过失，互有疏忽

contributory pension plan
分担退休基金办法

control
管制，控制，监督，检查，
核对

control account
统制账户

control key (ctrl) (c)
控制键（ctrl）

controllable costs
可控制成本

controlled company
受控制公司，分公司，
附属公司

controlled economy
统制经济

controller
总监，审计长

controlling interest
控股权，控制权

convenience sampling
便利抽样法

conventional mortgage
约定抵押，常规抵押

conversion
转化，变换，汇兑，
交换

- 30 -

conversion cost
转换成本，换算成本
conversion factor for employee contributions
员工贡献换算因子
conversion parity
兑换平价
conversion price
兑换价格，调换价格，汇价
conversion ratio
换算比率，兑换比率
convertibles
可兑换证券
convetible term life insurance
可转换定期人寿保险
convey
运送，转让，搬运，传达
conveyance
转让，运输，转让证书
cooling-off period
等待期，冷却期
co-op
消费合作社
cooperative
合作的，合作商店
cooperative advertising
合作广告，联合广告
cooperative apartment
共管公寓
copy-protected (c)
拷贝保护的，复制保护的

copyright
版权，著作权
cornering the market
垄断市场，囤积居奇
corporate bond
公司债
corporate campaign
公司公关活动
corporate equivalent yield
公司约当收益率
corporate strategic planning
公司战略计划
corporate structure
公司组织结构
corporate veil
以公司作掩护
corporation
公司，有限公司，股份公司
corporeal
物质的，有形的，标的物的
corpus
基金本金，主体财产
correction
市价上涨后的回落，调整，修正，纠正
correlation coefficient
相关系数
correspondent
顾客，往来客户，代理商行

corrupted (c)
被破坏的

cosign
联署

cost
成本，费用，价格

cost accounting
成本会计，
成本核算

cost application
成本摊派，
成本分配

cost approach
成本计算法

cost basis
成本基础

cost-benefit analysis
成本效益分析

cost center
成本中心

cost containment
成本限制

cost-effectiveness
成本效益，
成本效用

cost method
成本估计法

cost objective
成本对象，成本目标

cost of capital
资本成本

cost of carry
附加成本，折旧成本

cost of goods
manufactured
制成品成本

cost of goods sold
销售成本，销货成本

cost-of-living adjustment
(COLA)
生活费用调整
（COLA）

cost overrun
超额费用

cost-plus contract
成本附加合同

cost-push inflation
成本推动型通货膨胀

cost records
成本记录，成本登记

co-tenancy
共有物业

cottage industry
家庭手工业

counsel
辩护人，出庭律师，
法律顾问

counterclaim
反诉

countercycical
policy
反周期财政政策

counterfeit
伪造的，假冒的，伪币

countermand
取消，撤回，止付

counteroffer
反要约，还价

coupon bond
附息票债券

court of record
法庭记录

covariance
协方差

covenant
契约，条款，保护条款

covenant not to
compete
保证不竞争条款

cover
保险，承保，弥补，抵偿，
包括

covered option
有保证期权

cracker
换钞人，推销员

craft union
行业工会

crash
大跌，崩溃，破产
(c) 系统性故障，崩溃，
失效

creative black
book
创新型供应商黑皮书

creative financing
创造性融资安排

credit
信贷，信用，贷方，
信用证

credit analyst
信用分析师

credit balance
贷方节余，结欠

credit bureau
征信所，信用咨询公司

credit card
信用卡，转账卡

creditor
债权人

credit order
信用定单

credit rating
信用评级，
信用定额

crdit requirements
信贷要求

credit risk
信用风险

credit union
信用合作社

creeping inflation
潜行通货膨胀

critical path method
(CPM)
统筹法（CPM）

critical region
临界区域

crop (c)
修剪，剪切

cross
交叉，跨越

cross-footing
交叉总计

cross merchandising
交叉商品摆放

cross purchase plan
交叉购买计划

cross tabulation
交叉列表

crowd
到场参加交易的伙伴

crowding out
挤出，推出

crown jewels
最值钱部分

crown loan
克朗贷款

cum dividend, cum rights or cum warrant
有股息，附有权利或附带权利

cumulative dividend
累积股息

cumulative liability
累积责任

cumulative preferred stock
累积优先股

cumulative voting
累积投票权

curable depreciation
可挽回的贬值

currency futures
货币期货

currency in circulation
流通中的货币

current
活期，通用的，本期的，当前的

current asset
流动资产

current assumption whole life insurance
当前假定全寿命期保险

current cost
时价，本期成本

current dollars
现值美元

current liabilities
流动负债

current market value
当时市价

current ratio
现行比率

current valu accounting
现值会计法

current yield
本期收益

cursor (c)
光标

curtailment in pension plan
削减养老金计划

curtesy
鳏夫产权

curtilage
庭园，宅地

custodial account
保管账户

custodian
保管人，管理人

custody
保管，保护

customer
顾客，买方

customer profile
顾客群组特征

customer service
顾客服务

customer service representative
顾客服务代表

customs
海关，关税

customs court
海关法院

cutoff point
停止供应点，投资截点

cyberspace (c)
电脑空间

cycle billing
分期开列账单

cyclical demand
周期性需求

cyclical industry
周期性产业

cyclical stock
周期性产业股票

cyclical unemployment
周期性失业

cyclic variation
周期性变化

D

daily trading limit
每日交易极限

daisy chain
连接器，联手操盘托市

damages
损害，损失，赔偿金

data
资料，数据，事实，
知识

database
数据库

database management
数据库管理

data collection (c)
数据收集

data maintenance (c)
数据维护

data processing insurance
数据处理保险

data retrieval (c)
数据检索

data transmission (c)
数据传送

date of issue
发行日期，签发日期

date of record
记录日期，过户日期

dating
填日期，注明日期

deadbeat
故意赖账者

dead-end job
没有出路的工作

deadhead
免费乘客，免费入场者

deadline
截止日期

dead stock
滞销货，呆滞资金

dead time
窝工工时，停工时间

dealer
贩子，商人，经纪人

death benefit
死亡抚恤金

debasement
降低品质，贬值，
变质

debenture
债券，公司债券，
退税凭单

debit
借方，借入，欠债

debit memorandum
借项凭单，
欠款通知单

debt
债，欠债，欠款

debt coverage ratio
偿债能力系数

debt instrument
债券

debtor
债务人

debt retirement
偿债，偿还债务

debt security
债券

debt service
偿债，债务还本付息

debt-to-equity ratio
负债与股东权益比率

debug (c)
调试，除错

decentralization
分制权，分权管理，分散

deceptive advertising
欺骗性广告

deceptive packaging
欺骗性包装

decision model
决策模型

decision package
决策组，决策单元

decision support system (DSS)
决策支持系统

decision tree
决策树，决策体系

declaration
申请，申报，声明，宣布

declaration of estimated tax
估计税额申报

declaration of trust
信托声明

declare
申报，宣布，声明，表示，报关

declining-balance method
余额递减法

decryption (c)
解密，解码

dedicated line
专用线路

dedication
献地

deductibility of employee contributions
员工摊付款的可扣除性

deduction
扣除额，减免额，演绎

deductive reasoning
演绎推理

deed
契据，证书，契约

deed in lieu of foreclosure
替代没收的土地返还行为

deed of trust
信托契约

deed restriction
契约限制条款

deep discount bond
大幅度贴现债券

de facto corporation
实际公司

defalcation
盗用公款，侵吞

default
违约，不履行，缺省

default judgment
缺席判决

defeasance
作废，废除契约的条款

defective
有缺陷的，亏损的

defective title
有缺陷的产权

defendant
被告

defense of suit against insured
针对被保险人的诉讼辩护

defensive securities
防护性证券

deferred account
延期账，递延账户

deferred billing
延期开单

deferred charge
延期费

deferred compensation
递延补偿

deferred compensation plan
延期补偿计划

deferred contribution plan
延期摊付计划

deferred credit
递延贷款

deferred group annuity
递延集体年金

deferred interest bond
递延利息债券

deferred maintenance
递延维持费

deferred-payment annuity
延期付款年金

deferred payments
延期付款

deferred profit-sharing
延期利润分享

deferred retirement
递延退休

deferred retirement credit
递延贷款

deferred wage increase
递延工资增长

deficiency
亏损，不足额，缺少

deficiency judgment
补正判决

deficiency letter
补正通知单

deficit
亏损，亏空，逆差，赤字

deficit financing
赤字金融

deficit net worth
赤字资产净值

deficit spending
赤字开支，超支

defined-benefit pension plan
确定福利养老金计划

defined contributuion pension plan
确定养老金方案

deflation
通货紧缩

deflator
减缩指数，
通货膨胀扣除率

defunct compnay
已停业公司

degression
递减

deindustrialization
非工业化

delegate
代表，委托，委任

delete (c)
删除

delete key (del) (c)
删除键（del）

delinquency
拖欠债务，失职

delinquent
拖欠的，违约的，
失职的

delisting
除牌

delivery
交货，递交，投递

delivery date
交货期，交货日期

demand
要求，需求，申请

demand curve
需求曲线

demand deposit
即期存款，活期存款

demand loan
活期贷款

demand note
即期票据

demand price
需求价格

demand-pull inflation
需求扩大型通货膨胀

demand schedule
需求表

demarketing
低行销，反倾销

demised premises
已租让房产

demographics
人口统计

demolition
拆除

demonetization
非货币化

demoralize
使消沉，
使道德败坏

demurrage
滞留期，
延期停泊

demurrer
抗辩，异议

denomination
票面金额

density
密度，浓度**

density zoning
密度分区限制

department
部门

dependent
依靠的，相关的，
从属的

dependent coverage
受赡养人保险

depletion
折耗

deposit
存款，押金，存放

**deposit administration
plan**
存款管理计划

deposit in transit
在途存款

deposition
宣誓，作证

**depositors forgery
insurance**
存款人虚假保险

**depository trust company
(DTC)**
保管人信托公司（DTC）

depreciable life
应折旧年限

depreciable real estate
应折旧不动产

depreciate
折旧，贬值

depreciated cost
折余成本

depreciation
贬值，折旧

depreciation recapture
折旧回收

depreciation reserve
折旧准备

depression
萧条，衰退

depth interview
现场顾客深度调查

deregulation
解除管制

derived demand
衍生需求，引伸需求

descent
无遗嘱遗产

description
描述，说明

**descriptive
memorandum**
叙述性备忘录

descriptive statistics
叙述性统计

desk
工作台，服务台，
部

desktop publishing
桌面计算机排版系统

**destination file
(network) (c)**
目标文件

detail person
营销代表，
推销员

devaluation
货币贬值

developer
开发商

development
开发

developmental drilling program
开发性开采项目

development stage enterprise
草创阶段企业

deviation policy
脱规政策

devise
不动产遗赠，
发明

dialup
拨号

diangonal expansion
派生产品扩展

diary
日记

differential advantage
差别优势

differential analysis
差异分析

differentiation strategy
差别策略

digits deleted
被删除数字

dilution
冲淡，稀释

diminishing-balance method
余额递减折旧法

diplomacy
外交，外交手腕

direct access
直接存取，直接作业

direct-action advertising
直接行动广告

direct charge-off method
直接冲销法

direct cost
直接成本

direct costing
直接成本法

direct verdict
直接裁决

direct financing lease
直接融资租赁

direct investment
直接投资

direct labor
直接人工成本

direct liability
直接负债

direct marketing
直接营销

direct material
直接原料成本

director
董事，主任，管理者

directorate
董事会，理事会

direct overhead
直接管理费用

direct-reduction mortgage
本息同时扣除抵押贷款

direct response advertising
直接反应广告

direct sales
直接销售

direct production
直接生产

disability benefit
伤残恤养金

disability buy-out insurance
伤残买断保险

disability income insurance
伤残收入保险

disaffirm
反驳，否认

disbursement
支出，付款

discharge
卸货，解除，释放

discharge in bankruptcy
解除破产债务

discharge in lien
解除留置权

disciplinary layoff
惩戒性临时解雇

disclaimer
弃权，否认，不承认，不认领

disclosure
揭示，透露，表述

discontinuance of plan
计划中断

discontinued operation
停产，停售

discount
贴现，折扣

discount bond
贴现债券

discount broker
票据贴现经纪人

discounted cash flow
折现现金流量

discounting the news
根据预期消息开价

discount points
贴现点数

discount rate
贴现率

discount window
贴现贷款业务窗口

discount yield
贴现收益率

discovery
发现，披露

discovery sampling
发现采样

discrepancy
不一致，差异

discretion
自行处理

discretionary cost
任意性成本，自定成本

discretionary income
可自由支配的收入

discretionary policy
可自由处理的政策

discretionary spending power
收入中可自由支配的购买力

discrimination
歧视，区别

diseconomies
不经济，成本的增加

dishonor
拒绝付款，拒绝承兑

disinflation
通货收缩，反通货膨胀

disintermediation
不干预

disjoint events
不相交事件

disk (c)
磁盘

disk drive (c)
磁盘机，磁盘驱动器

dismissal
免职，解雇，开除

dispatcher
调度员，发送人

disposable income
可支配收入

dispossess
驱逐，剥夺，撵走

dispossess proceedings
驱逐行动

dissolution
解除，解体，溶解

distressed property
被扣押财产

distribution
分配，分布，分销，
推销，流通，配载

distribution allowance
分销折扣

distribution cost analysis
分配成本分析，
推销费用分析

distributor
经销者，发行人，批发商

diversification
多样化，分散经营

diversified company
多种经营公司

divestiture
剥夺

dividend
红利，股利，股息

dividend addition
股息附加

dividend exclusion
股息不予计列

dividend payout ratio
股息分配率

dividend reinvestment plan
股息再投资计划

dividend requirement
派息要求

dividend rollover plan
股息贷款计划

dividends payable
应付未付股息

division of labor
分工

docking
缺勤费

docking station (c)
坞站

documentary evidence
书面证据，证明文件

documentation
提示单证，证明文件

doing business as (DBA)
假定商业名称

dollar cost averaging
美元成本平均

dollar drain
美元枯竭

dollar unit sampling (DUS)
美元单位采样
（DUS）

dollar value lifo
美元币值后进先出法

domain name system
域名系统

domestic corporation
国内公司

domicile
住所，期票支付场所

dominant tenement
主要地产

donated stock
捐赠股份

donated surplus
捐赠盈余

donor
捐款人，捐赠人

double click (c)
双击

double declining balance
双倍余额递减法

double-digit inflation
两位数的通货膨胀

double-dipping
双重职业

double-entry accounting
复式会计

double precision
双精度

double taxation
双重征税

double time
双倍加班费

double (treble) damages
双倍（三倍）损失补偿

dower
亡夫遗产

download (c)
下载

downpayment
预付款,
分期付款定金

downscale
缩减规模

downside risk
下降风险

downstream
后续程序

down tick
向下赊购

downtime
准备时间，停工时间

downturn
下跌，下降趋势

downzoning
下降分带

dowry
嫁妆

dow theory
道氏理论

draft
汇票，付款通知，草案,
选拔

draining reserves
外流储备

draw
支取，提款，预支佣金，借款

draw tool (c)
画线工具

drawee
汇票受票人，付款人

drawer
出票人

drawing account
提款账户，提存账户

drive (c)
驱动，推动

drop-down menu (pull-down menu) (c)
下拉式选项屏
(下拉式选单)

drop-shipping
直接运输，直达货运

dry goods
绸缎，呢绒类，
布匹织物类

dual contract
复式合约

due bill
到期票据，借据

due-on-sale clause
销售后贷款立即到位条款

dummy
虚假物，虚拟

dumping
倾销

dun
讨债，催债

duplex copying (printing) (c)
双面拷贝（打印）

duplication of benefits
福利重叠

duress
强迫，胁迫

dutch auction
荷兰式拍卖

duty
税，关税，责任

E

each way
买卖双方个别负担之约定

early retirement
提早退休

early retirement benefits
提前退休金

early withdrawal penalty
提前支取罚款

earned income
劳力收入

earnest money
定金，保证金

earnings and profits
收入及收益

earnings before taxs
税前收益

earnings per share
每股收益

earnings report
收益报告

easement
地役权

easy money
放松银根，低利贷款，低息货币

econometrics
计量经济学

economic
经济的，经济学的

economic analysis
经济分析

economic base
经济基础

economic depreciation
经济性贬值，由外在原因引起的地产贬值

economic freedom
经济自由

economic growth
经济增长

economic growth rate
经济增长率

economic indicators
经济指标

economic life
经济寿命

economic loss
经济损失

economic rent
经济租金

economics
经济学

economic sanctions
经济制裁

economic system
经济制度

economic value
经济价值

economies of scale
规模经济

economist
经济学家

economy
经济

edit (c)
编辑

effective date
生效日期，有效日期

effective debt
有效债务

effective net worth
有效资产净值

effective rate
实际利率

effective tax rate
实际税率

efficiency
有效性，效率

efficient market
有效市场

efficient portfolio
有效有价证券

eject (c)
退出，弹出

ejectment
驱逐，收回不动产（地产占有权）诉讼

elasticity of supply and demand
供求弹性

elect
选择

electronic mail (email)
电子邮件（EMAIL）

eligibility requirements
资格要求

eligible paper
合法证券

email address
电子邮件地址

emancipation
自立，解放，释放

embargo
封港，禁运

embed (c)
嵌入

embezzlement
侵吞，贪污，监守自盗，挪用公款

emblement
耕作的庄稼，庄稼收益

eminent domain
征用权，国家征用私产权

employee
职工，雇员，员工

employee association
雇员协会

employee benefits
员工福利

employee contributions
雇员醵出金，员工摊款

employee profit sharing
员工福利分享

employee stock option
职工认股权

employee stock ownership plan (ESOP)
职工股票所有权计划

employer
雇主，业主

employer interference
雇主干涉

employment agency
职业介绍所

employment contract
聘约，雇用合同

enable (c)
启动，允许，使能，
激活

enabling clause
授权法案

encoding
加密

encroach
侵占，侵犯

encroachment
侵占，侵犯

encryption
加密

encumbrance
债权，财产置留权

end of month
月底

end user (c)
最终用户

endorsement or
indorsement
背书

endowment
捐赠，捐款

energy tax credit
能源税信贷

enjoin
责成，指示

enterprise
企业，事业，公司

enterprise zone
保税区

entity
实体，机构

entreprenuer
企业家

entry-level job
入门性工作

environmental impact
satement (eis)
环境影响报告

eom dating
月底付账法

equalization board
统一地税委员会

equal opportunity
employer
倡导就业机会均等的雇主

equal protection of the
laws
法律平等保护权

equilibrium
平衡，均衡

equilibrium price
均衡价格

equilibrium quantity
均衡数量

equipment
设备，装备，
器材

equipment leasing
设备租赁

equipment trust bond
设备信托债券

equitable
公正的，公平的

equitable distribution
公平分配

equity
权益，产权，股权，股票，
证券

equity financing
增股筹资

equity method
净值法，产权法

equity of redemption
衡平偿还权

equity reit
业主权

equivalent taxable yield
约当可征税收益

erase (c)
清除，删除

error
错误，差错

error message (c)
错误信息

escalator clause
调整条款

escape key (esc) (c)
换码键

escheat
无继承人的财产，
产业归公

escrow
附条件委付盖印契约（由
第三者保存，待条件完成
后即交受让人的契据）

escrow agent
委付代理

espionage
间谍活动

essential industry
基础产业，主要产业

estate
财产，房地产，所有权

estate in reversion
可期待继承的遗产

estate in severalty
独占的不动产

estate planning
财产规划

estate tax
遗产税

estimate
估计，预计

estimated tax
估计税款

estimator
估价员，概算员

estoppel
禁止翻供

estoppel certificate
禁止翻供证明

estovers
必需品

ethical, ethics
道德，伦理

euro
欧元

European Common
Market
欧洲共同市场

European Economic
Community (EEC)
欧洲经济共同体（EEC）

eviction
收回租地，逐出

eviction, actual
实际驱逐

eviction, constructive
推定驱逐

eviction, partial
部分驱逐

evidence of title
所有权证明

exact interest
实计利息，抽息

"except for" opinion
查账附注意见

excess profits tax
超额利得税

excess reserves
超额储备金

exchange
交换，交易，汇票，
交易所

exchange control
外汇管制

exchange rate
汇率，汇价

excise tax
消费税，货物税

exclusion
排斥，排除

exclusion clause
（保险契约中声明）
的除外条款

exculpatory
抗辩，辩护

ex-dividend date
除息日期

execute
履行，实施，执行，转让

executed
已履行

executed contract
已履行合同

execution
实行，执行，履行，
签名生效

executive
执行的，行政的，
主管人员，经理

executive committee
执行委员会

executive
perquisites
公司高级主管人员待遇

executor
执行者，遗嘱执行人

executory
待执行的

exemption
免税，豁免，免税额，
除外

exempt securities
免办登记证券

exercise
运用，履行，实习

exit interview
离职面谈

ex-legal
未印法律意见的债券

expandable (c)
可扩充的

expansion
扩建，扩张

expected value
预期值，期望值

expense
经费，花费

expense account
费用账户，支出账户

expense budget
费用预算

expense ratio
费用比率

expense report
费用报告

experience refund
再保经验退还金

experience rating
经验定额，
经验费率

expert power
专家权威

expiration
到期，有效期，终止

expiration notice
到期通知

exploitation
剥削，开发，利用

exponential smoothing
指数平滑法

export
出口，出口额，出口商品

export-import bank
(eximbank)
美国进出口银行（EXIM）

exposure
风险，揭露，广告暴露程
度，方位

exposure draft
征询意见稿

express
表达，快运汇，捷运公司

express authority
明示权限

express contract
明示合同

extended coverage
扩展保险范围

extended coverage
endorsement
扩展保险范围批单

extension
延期，扩展，延长期

extension of time for filing
延长报税截止期

extenuating circumstances
可斟酌的情形，情有可原

external audit
外界审计

external documents
外部文件

external funds
外部资金

external report
对外报告

extractive industry
采掘工业，提炼工业

extra dividend
特别红利，额外股息

extraordinary dividends
非经常性股息

extraordinary item
特殊项目，非经常性项目

extrapolation
外推法

F

fabricator
装配工

face amount
面额

face interest rate
票面利率

face value
面值

facility
熟练，设备，工具，便利

facsimile
传真

factor analysis
因素分析

factorial
阶乘积，析因，
阶乘

factoring
财务代理商，
托收信贷行

factory overhead
间接制造费用

fail to deliver
未能支付

fail to receive
未能接收

failure analysis
失败分析

fair market rent
公平市场租金

fair market value
公平市价

fair rate of return
公平报酬率

fair trade
互惠贸易，公平交易

fallback option
后备选择权

fallen building clause
倒坍房屋条款

false advertising
虚假广告

family income policy
家庭收入保险单

family life cycle
家庭寿命周期

family of funds
基金组合

FAQ (frequently asked
questions) (c)
常见问题（经常问到的问题）

farm surplus
剩余农产品

fascism
法西斯主义

fast tracking
快速培养

fatal error (c)
致命错误

faulty installation
有缺陷的安装

favorable trade balance
贸易顺差

feasibility study
可行性研究

featherbedding
额外雇工，强迫雇用

federal deficit
联邦赤字

Federal Deposit Insurance Corporation (FDIC)
联邦储蓄保险公司
（FDIC）

federal funds
联邦资金

federal funds rate
联邦资金利率

Federal Reserve Bank
联邦储备银行

Federal Reserve Board (FRB)
联邦储备局（FRB）

Federal Reserve System (FED)
联邦储备系统

Federal Savings and Loan Association
联邦储备及贷款协会

fed wire
联邦储蓄银行通讯网络

fee
费，费用，手续费，税，小账

feeder lines
补给线

fee simple or fee simple absolute
土地绝对所有权

FHA motgage loan
由联邦房屋管理局提供保险的抵押贷款

fidelity bond
忠实保证，员工信用保证

fiduciary
信托的，信托者

fiduciary bond
受托人保证

field staff
现场工作人员

field theory of motivation
现场激励理论

file
文件，档案

file backup (c)
文件备份

file extension (c)
文件扩充

file format (c)
文件格式

file transfer protocol (FTP) (c)
文件传输协议（FTP）

fill or kill (FOK)
指令立即买卖某一证券，成交或取消（FOK）

filtering down
最终渗透

final assembly
总装，最后装配

finance charge
信贷延期费

finance company
信贷公司,
金融公司

financial accounting
财务会计

financial advertising
财务广告

financial future
金融期货

financial insitution
金融机构

financial intermediary
金融中介

financial lease
金融租赁

financial management rate
of return (FMRR)
金融管理回报率 (FMRR)

financial market
金融市场

financial position
财务状况

financial pyramid
财务金字塔风险结构

financial statement
财务报表

financial stucture
财务结构

financial supermarket
金融超市

financing
融资, 筹资

finder's fee
中间人佣金

finished goods
制成品

fire insurance
火灾保险

firm
公司, 商号, 厂商

firm commitment
债券的总额承受,
包销承诺, 包销

firm offer
实盘, 确盘

firm order
确定订货

firm quote
确定报价

first in, first out (FIFO)
先进先出 (FIFO)

first lien
最先留置权

first-line management
基层管理部门

first mortgage
第一抵押权

first-year depreciation
第一年折旧

fiscal
财政的, 国库的, 会计的

fiscal agent
财务代理人

fiscalist
主张政府影响经济运行的
经济学家

fiscal policy
财政政策

fixation
固定, 决定

fixed annuity
固定年金

fixed asset
固定资产

fixed benefits
固定福利

fixed charge
固定费用，固定支出

fixed-charge coverage
固定费用负担保障

fixed cost
固定成本

fixed fee
固定收费

fixed income
固定收入

fixed income statement
固定收入损益表

fixed-point number
定点数

fixed premium
固定保费

fixed-price contract
固定价格合同

fixed-rate loan
固定利率贷款

fixture
过时货，装置物

flanker brand
延展品牌

flash memory (c)
快速[闪]存储器

flat
平坦，平展的，恰好，价格平稳，无息的

flat rate
统一费率，定额

flat scale
统一工时费

flat tax
单一税率

flexible budget
弹性预算

flexible-payment mortgage (FPM)
弹性付款抵押贷款（FPM）

flextime
弹性工作制

flight to quality
追求投资质量

float
浮动，发行，创立

floater
证券保险

floating debt
流动负债

floating currency exchange rate
浮动货币汇率

floating exchange rate
浮动汇率

floating-point number
浮点数

floating-rate note
浮动利率票据

floating securities
浮动证券

floating supply
流动供应

flood insurance
水灾险

floor loan
最低贷款额

floor plan
楼层布局

floor plan insurance
铺面保险

flotation (floatation) cost
发行成本

flowchart
流程图，程序表

flow of funds
资金流量

fluctuation
变动，浮动，起伏

fluctuation limit
浮动限幅

flush (left/right) (c)
(左/右边)排齐

follow-up letter
后续营销信

font (c)
字型，字体，字模

footing
总结，结算，英尺，合计

footnote (c)
脚注

forced page break (c)
强制换页

forced sale
强制出售，迫卖

forced saving
强制储蓄

forecasting
预测

foreclosure
取消抵押品赎回权

foreign corporation
外国公司

foreign direct investment
国外直接投资

foreign exchange
外汇

foreign income
国外收入

foreign investment
国外投资，外商投资

foreign trade zone
外贸区

forfeiture
没收，罚款

forgery
伪造签字或文件

format (c)
格式，格式化

formula investing
公式投资，方案投资

fortuitous loss
意外损失

forward
远期，期货

forward contract
期货合同，
远期合同

forwarding company
转运公司

forward integration
远期合并

forward pricing
远期定价

forward stock
待售商品，
期货证券

for your information (FYI)
仅供参考（FYI）

foul bill of lading
不洁提单

401(k) plan
401（K）方案

fourth market
第四市场

fractional share
零星股份，
不足额股份

frame rate (c)
帧速率

franchise
免赔额，特许证书，特许权，选举权

franchise tax
特许经营税，专卖税

frank
免费邮寄，邮资先付

fraud
欺骗，欺诈

fraudulent misrepresentation
虚假的陈述

free alongside ship (FAS)
船边交货价，靠船价

free and clear
自由处理

free and open market
自由开放市场

free enterprise
自由企业

freehold (estate)
（地产）自由保有权

free market
自由市场

free on board (FOB)
离岸价格（FOB）

free port
自由港，免税港

freight insurance
运费保险

frequency
次数，频率，频数，广告频率

frictional unemployment
短期失业

friendly suit
友好诉讼

frontage
前面或正面的长度

front-end load
前端负载

front foot
前面长度

front money
预付定金

front office
董事会，理事会，全体决策人员

frozen account
冻结账户

F statistic
F 值统计

fulfillment
履行，完成

full coverage
完全承保，
全面保险

full disclosure
财务公开

full faith and credit
市政信用

full screen display (c)
全屏幕显示

full-service broker
全面服务经纪人

fully diluted earnings per (common) share
全面冲淡每（普通）股赢利

fully paid policy
完全付清保单

functional authority
职能权力

functional currency
功能性货币

functional obsolescence
功能性萎缩

fuctional organization
职能部门

function key (c)
功能键

fund accounting
基金会计

fundamental analysis
基本分析

funded debt
长期债务

funded pension plan
设有基金的退休计划

funding
筹集资金，债务转期

fund-raising
资金筹措

furlough
休假

future interest
将来利息

futures contract
期货合同

futures market
期货市场

G

gain
收益，利益，利润，
增加

gain contingency
收益可能性

galloping inflation
急剧的通货膨胀

game card (c)
游戏卡

gaming
博弈，赌博

gap
亏空，不足，短缺

gap loan
缺口资金贷款

garnish
装饰，修饰，扣押

garnishee
第三债务人，传讯，
扣押

garnishment
扣押被告财产的通知，
扣押令

gender analysis
性别分析

general contractor
总合同

general equilibrium
analysis
一般均衡分析

general expense
一般费用，日用开支，
杂费

general fund
普通基金

generalist
多面手，通才

general journal
普通日记账，普通分录账

general ledger
总分类账

general liability insurance
一般责任险

general lien
一般留置权

generally accepted
accounting principles
公认会计原则

general obligation
bond
普通责任债务

general partner
普通合伙人

general revenue
一般收入

general revenue
sharing
一般收入分享

general scheme
一般投递流程

general strike
总罢工

general warranty deed
全面保证书

generation-skipping transfer
隔代财产转移

generic appeal
泛指广告

generic bond
一般债券

generic market
广泛市场

gentrification
住宅区阶层上移

geodemography
地域人口统计学

gift
礼品，赠品，授予权，赠送

gift deed
赠与行为

gift tax
赠与税

girth
横梁

glamor stock
热门股票

glut
供过于求

goal
终点，目标，标的

goal congruence
目标一致性

goal programming
目标规划

goal setting
目标设定

go-between
中间人，经纪人

going-concern value
继续经营条款

going long
买空

going private
私人投资，不公开买卖

going public
公众投资，公开买卖

going short
卖空

goldbrick
假金砖，赝品，假货

goldbug
臭财主，主张金本位者

golden handcuffs
以公司股票吸引主要员工的方法

golden handshake
提前退休奖励计划

golden parachute
公司高层福利合同

gold fixing
议定金价

gold mutual fund
黄金互助资金

gold standard
金本位

good delivery
完好交货

good faith
信誉

good-faith deposit
意向订金，善意保证金

good money
高薪，巨款

goodness-of-fit test
适合性检验

goods
货物，商品，货品

goods and services
商品与劳务

good-till-canceled order (GTC)
按指定价格进行交易 （GTC）

good title
有效的所有权

goodwill
商誉，信誉

grace period
宽限期，优惠期

graduated lease
分级租赁

graph (c)
图，图形

graphics card (c)
图形卡

gratuated payment mortgage (GPM)
分级支付抵押贷款 （GPM）

gratuated wage
分级工资

graft
贪污，受贿

grandfather clause
不追溯条款

grant
许可，授予，让予， 转让证书

grantee
被授与者，受让人

grantor
授与者，转让人

grantor trust
转让人信托

gratis
无偿

gratuitous
无偿的

gratuity
小账，赏金，抚恤金

graveyard market
濒死股市

graveyard shift
夜班

gray scale (c)
灰度

great depression
大萧条

greenmail
绿色收购，被收购公司以 市场价转让股票的安排

gross
全体，总计，毛额，毛重

gross amount
总额，总计

gross billing
总通讯费

gross earnings
总收入，毛利

gross estate
总资产

gross income
总收入

gross leaseable area
可出租总面积

gross lease
全包出租

gross national debt
国民负债总额

gross national expenditure
国民支出总值

gross national product
(GNP)
国民生产总值

gross profit
毛利润，总利润

gross profit method
毛利法，总利润法

gross profit ratio
毛利率，总利润比率

gross rating point (GRP)
按毛费率计算（GRP）

gross rent multiplier
(GRM)
毛租金倍数（GRM）

gross revenue
收入总额

gross ton
英吨

gross weight
总重，毛重，全重

ground lease
地契

ground rent
地租

group credit insurance
团体信用保险

group disability insurance
团体伤残险

group health insurance
团体健康保险

group life insurance
团体人寿保险

growing-equity mortgage
(GEM)
不断增长产权长期抵押贷款

growth fund
发展基金

growth rate
增长率，成长率

growth stock
增长股份，成长股

guarantee
保证，担保，保证书

guaranteed annual wage
(GAW)
年保证工资

guaranteed bond
担保债券

guaranteed income
contract (GIC)
保证收入合同（GIC）

guaranteed insurability
保证可保险性

guaranteed mortgage
保证抵押贷款

guaranteed security
保证证券

guaranteed letter
保证书

guarantee of signature
签字真实性保证

guarantor

保证人，担保人

guaranty

保证书，抵押品

guardian

管理人，监护人

guardian deed

监护人行为

guideline lives

标准使用年限

guild

行会，同业公会

H

habendum
受让人及受让地产定义条款

hacker
骇客，计算机程序专家

half duplex
半双向

half-life
半衰期，半减期

halo effect
光环效应

hammering the market
大量抛售股票

handling allowance
产品整理折扣

hangout
贷款余额

hard cash
硬币，现金

hard currency
硬通货，硬币，紧俏货币

hard disk (c)
硬盘

hard dollars
实际付款

hard drive (c)
硬盘驱动器

hard goods
耐用货物

hard money
硬币，现金，硬通货，紧俏货币

hard return (c)
硬回车

hardware (c)
硬件

hardwired (c)
电路的，硬连线的

hash total
混列总量

hatch (c)
阴影线

hazard insurance
危害保险

head and shoulders
头肩形

header (c)
标题，报头

headhunter
私人职业介绍所

head of household
户主

health maintenance organization (HMO)
健康维护组织（HMO）

hearing
听证

heavy industry
重工业

hectare
公顷

hedge
对冲买卖，套期保值

heirs
继承人

heirs and assigns
继承人和受让人

help index (c)
求助信息索引

help screen (c)
求助屏幕

help wizard (c)
求助向导系统

heterogeneous
异质，多元

heuristic
启发式

hidden agenda
隐蔽日程

hidden asset
隐匿资产

hidden inflation
隐蔽性通货膨胀

hidden tax
隐蔽税收

hierarchy
分层，等级制度，级别，系统

high credit
高档信贷

highest and best use
最佳利用

high flyer
价格飞涨的存货，投机性股票

high-grade bond
高级债券

high-involvement model
高难度模型

highlight (c)
增亮，加亮

high resolution (c)
高分辨率

high-speed (c)
高速

highs
股票冲高值

high technology
高技术

high-tech stock
高技术公司股票

historical cost
历史成本，实际成本

historical yield
历史产率，实际收益率

historical structure
历史结构

hit list
目标客户名单

hit the bricks
员工罢工

hobby loss
由非盈利性爱好引起的损失，嗜好损失

holdback
暂欠，暂时扣发

holdback pay
暂欠工资

holder in due course
正当持票人

- 65 -

holder of record
记录在案的公司证券拥有
人

hold-harmless agreements
免损害协议

hold harmless clause
免损害条款

holding
把握，占有，存款，
所有物

holding company
控股公司

holding fee
储存费，保管费

holding period
持有期间

holdover tenant
赖住租户

home key (c)
(光标)返回原址键

homeowner's association
屋主协会

**homeowner's equity
account**
屋主产权账户

homeowner's policy
屋主保险单

**homeowner warranty
program (HOW)**
屋主担保计划（HOW）

home page (c)
主页，起始页

homestead
家宅，宅地

homestead tax exemption
宅地税务免除

homogeneous
同质的，同种类的

homogeneous oligopoly
同质垄断

honor
承付，承兑，付款，荣誉

honorarium
报酬金

horizontal analysis
横向分析

**horizontal channel
integration**
横向企业合并

horizontal combination
横向合并，同业联合

horizontal expansion
横向发展

horizontal merger
横向合并，同行业合并

horizontal specialization
横向专业分工

horizontal union
同业工会，
行业工会

host computer (c)
主机

hot cargo
热门货物

hot issue
热门股票

hot stock
热门股票

house
场所，机构，号子

house account
大客户

house to house
挨户服务

house-to-house sampling
挨家挨户派发样品

house-to-house selling
挨家挨户推销

housing bond
住宅债券

housing code
住宅建设规范

housing starts
新开工住宅数

huckster
沿街贩卖者

human factors
人为因素

human relations
人事关系，人际关系

human resource accouting
人力资源会计

human resources
人力资源

human resources management (HRM)
人力资源管理（HRM）

hurdle rate
设定利率

hush money
贿赂，贿赂金

hybrid annuity
混合年金

hyperinflation
恶性通货膨胀

hyperlink (c)
超级链接

hypertext
超文本

hypothecate
抵押，担保

hypothesis
假设，猜测，
前提

hypothesis testing
假设检验

I

icon
图标

ideal capacity
理想生产能力

idle capacity
闲置生产能力

illegal dividend
非法分红

illiquid
资金周转困难的公司，
非流动资产

image (c)
图象，影象，
映象

image advertising
形象广告

image definition (c)
图象定义

image file (c)
图象文件

impacted area
受影响地区

impaired capital
资本不足，
削弱的资本

impasse
僵局

imperfect market
不完全市场

imperialism
帝国主义

implied
默示的

implied contract
默约，默示合同

implied easement
默示地役权

implied in fact contract
事实上默认的合同

implied warranty
默示担保

import
进口，输入

import quota
进口配额

imposition
缴税，税款

impound
扣押，没收

impound account
储备金账户

imprest fund, imprest
system
定额储备金，定额备用金制

improved land
熟地，已开发土地

improvement
改良，改善

- 68 -

improvements and betterments insurance
装修改建保险

imputed cost
假设成本，归宿成本，估算成本

imputed income
应计收入，估算收入

imputed interest
应计利息，估算利息

imputed value or imputed income
估算价值或估算收入

inactive stock or inactive bond
呆滞股票或呆滞证券

inadvertently
疏忽的，非有意的

incapacity
无能，丧失能力

incentive fee
奖励费

incentive pay
奖金

incentive wage plan
奖励工资计划

incentive stock option (ISO)
奖励性股票认购权（ISO）

inchoate
空白汇票

incidental damages
附带损失，杂项损失

income
收入，收益，所得

income accounts
收益账户，损益账户

income approach
收入法，收益法

income averaging
收入平均法

income bond
收益债券

income effect
收入效应

income group
收入组别

income in respect of a decedent
死者的持续收入

income property
收入财产

income redistribution
收入再分配

income replacement
折合收入

income splitting
收入分析

income statement
收益表，损益表

income stream
收入流

income tax
所得税

income tax return
所得税报税单

incompatible (c)
不相容的，不兼容的

incompetent
无管辖权，无能力

incontestable clause
不可抗辩条款

inconvertible money
不能兑现的货币，
不兑换货币

incorporate
注册公司，附加

incorporation
成立公司，登记，有限公司

inncorporeal property
无形财产

incremental analysis
增量分析

incremental cash flow
增加现金流动

incremental spending
增量花费

incurable depreciation
不可挽回的折旧

indemnify
补偿，赔偿，使免于受罚，
保护

indemnity
赔偿，赔偿金，赔款

indent (c)
缩进编排

indenture
双联合同，契约

independence
独立，自主权

independent adjuster
独立理赔员

independent contractor
独立承包商

independent store
独立商店

independent union
独立工会

independent variables
自变量

indeterminate premium life insurance
无定额保费人寿保险

index
指数，指标，目录

indexation
指数化

index basis
指数基准

indexed life insurance
指数化人寿保险

indexed loan
指数化贷款

index fund
指数证券投资基金

indexing
指数调整

index lease
指数租赁

index options
股票指数选择权

indirect cost
间接成本

indirect labor
间接人工成本

indirect overhead
间接费用

indirect production
间接生产

individual bargaining
个别谈判，个别议价

individual life insurance
个人人寿保险

individual retirement
account (IRA)
个人退休金账户（IRA）

inductive reasoning
归纳推理

industrial
工业的，工业股票，
工业公司

industrial advertising
工业广告

industrial consumer
工业消费者

industrial engineer
工业工程师

industrial fatigue
工业性疲劳

industrial goods
工业品，工业用品

industrialist
实业家，企业家

industrial park
工业区

industrial production
工业生产

industrial property
工业产权

industrial psychology
工业心理学

industrial relations
企业关系

industrial revolution
工业革命

industrial union
工会

industry
工业，实业，行业，产业

industry standard
工业标准

inefficiency in the market
无效率市场

infant industry argument
幼稚工业保护说

inferential statistics
推理统计

inferior good
低档货，次品

inferred authority
递补职权

inflation
通货膨胀

inflation accounting
通货膨胀会计

inflationary gap
通货膨胀差额

inflationary spiral
螺旋式通货膨胀

inflation endorsement
通货膨胀附加条款

inflation rate
通货膨胀率

informal leader
非正式领袖

information flow (c)
信息流程，信息流

information page (c)
信息页

information return
信息申报表

infrastructure
基础设施

infringement
违约，侵犯，违反

ingress and egress
入境及出境权

inherent explosion clause
固有爆炸因素保险条款

inherit
继承

inheritance
继承权

inheritance tax
遗产税

in-house
内部的，对内的

initial public offering (IPO)
原始公开股（IPO）

initiative
积极性

injunction
禁令

injunction bond
禁令保证金

injury independent of all other means
独立工伤

inland carrier
内陆承运人

inner city
内陆城市

innovation
革新，创新，竞争

in perpetuity
永久所有权

input (c)
输入

input field (c)
输入字段，输入区

input mask (c)
输入掩码

input-output device (c)
输入-输出设备

inside information
内部消息

inside lot
中间地段

insider
内线，内部人员

insolvency
无力还债，破产

insolvency clause
破产条款

inspection
检查，检验

installation (c)
安装

installment
分期付款

installment contract
分期付款契约

installment sale
分期付款销售

institutional investor
投资法团，
投资机构

institutional lender
机构借款人

instrument
有价证券票据，工具，
文件，证书，契约

instrumentalities of transportation
运输工具

instrumentalitity
手段，工具，债券，票据，
文件，契约

insurability
可保险性

insurable interest
可保险利益

insurable title
可保险产权

insurance
保险，保单，保费，投保

insurance company
(insurer)
保险公司（保险人）

insurance contract
保险合同

insurance coverage
保险范围

insurance settlement
保险处理

insured
被保险人

insured account
被保险人账户

insurgent
反叛者

intangible asset
无形资产

intangible reward
无形报酬

intangible value
无形价值

integrated circuit
集成电路

integration, backward
反向联合

integration, forward
前向联合

integration, horizontal
横向联合

integration, vertical
竖向联合

integrity
完全性，完整性，诚实，
正直

interactive (c)
交互式的，人机对话的

interactive system
交互式系统

interest
利息，利益，权益，股权，
产权

interest group
利益集团

interest-only loan
只付利息的贷款

interest rate
利率

interest sensitive policies
利率敏感保险单

interface
界面

interim audit
年中审计，期中审计

interim financing
中期贷款

interim statement
期中报表

interindustry
competition
产业部门间竞争，
工业间竞争

interlocking directorate
交叉董事会，
互兼董事

interlocutory decree
临时判决

intermediary
中间人，居间人

intermediate goods
中间货物，中间产品

intermediate term
中期

intermediation
中介作用，媒介作用

intermittent production
间歇性生产

internal audit
内部审计

internal check
内部检查，内部审核

internal control
内部控制，内部管理

internal expansion
内部资产扩充

internal financing
内部融资

internal memory (c)
内存(储器)

internal modem (c)
内置式调制解调器

internal rate of return (IRR)
内部利润率（IRR）

Internal Revenue Service (IRS)
美国税务总局
（IRS）

International Bank for Reconstruction and Development (IBRD)
国际开发银行

international cartel
国际卡特尔

international law
国际法

International Monetary Fund (IMF)
国际货币基金

International Monetary Market (IMM)
国际货币市场

international union
国际联盟

internet
互联网

internet protocol (IP) address
互联网协议（IP）地址

internet service provider
互联网服务提供商

interperiod income tax allocation
年度间所得税分配

interpleader
相互诉讼者

interpolation
插值法

interpreter
口译，翻译

interrogatories
询问

interval scale
区间尺度

interview
访谈，面谈

interview, structured
正式面谈

interview, unstructured
非正式面谈

interviewer bias
调查者偏倚

intestate
未留下遗嘱的，无遗嘱死亡者

in the money
资金充裕，较现值有利

in the tank
缺乏客观性

intraperiod tax allocation
期内所得税分摊

intrinsic value
本质价，固有价值

inure
生效，适用

inventory
库存，盘点，商品目录，清单

inventory certificate
库存证书

inventory contol
库存控制

inventory financing
以存货融通资金

inventory planning
库存规划

inventory shortage (shrinkage)
存货盘亏，存货短缺

inventory turnover
存货周转

inverse condemnation
反向谴责

inverted yield curve
反向产率曲线

invest
投资，投入

investment
投资，投入资本，资本

investment advisory service
投资咨询服务

investment banker
投资银行家

investment club
投资俱乐部

investment company
投资公司

investment counsel
投资顾问

investment grade
投资等级

investment interest expense
投资利息支出

investment life cycle
投资循环期

investment strategy
投资策略

investment trust
投资信托

investor relations department
投资人联络部

invoice
发票，货物托运单

involuntary conversion
非自愿转换

involuntary lien
非自愿留置

involuntary trust
非自愿信托

involuntary unemployment
非自愿失业

inwood annuity factor
因伍德年金因子

iota
很小数量，极微小

irregulars
不合格品，劣品

irreparable harm, irreparable damage
不可弥补的伤害，不可弥补的损坏

irretrievable (c)
无法检索的

irrevocable
不可撤消的

irrevocable trust
不可撤消信托

issue
开发，发行，争议的问题，纠纷

issued and outstanding
发行在外的股票

issuer
开证银行，证券发行者

itemized deductions
法定扣减项目

iteration
重复操作，重复运算

itinerant worker
流动工人

J

jawboning
赊买，借贷
J-curve
J曲线
job
工作，职位，任务，
批发
job bank
工作职位资料库
jobber
计件工，临时工，
股票公司，批发商
job classification
职业分类
job cost sheet
分批成本单
job depth
工作深度
job description
职责
job evaluation
工作评价
job jumper
跳槽者
job lot
分批出售，批量
job order
分批工作通知单，
订货，定单

job placement
工作安排
job rotation
工作轮换
job satisfaction
工作满意度
job security
工作稳定性
job sharing
工作共享
job shop
小批量生产厂家
job specification
工作说明书，操作规程
job ticket
工作卡片
joint account
共同账户
joint and several liability
连带责任
joint and survivor annuity
联合生存者年金
joint fare, joint rate
联合票价
joint liability
连带责任，共同负责
jointly and severally
共同及个别责任者

joint product cost
联产品成本

joint return
联合税务申报

joint stock company
股份公司

joint tenancy
联合租借，
共有不动产权

joint venture
合资企业

journal
日记账，流水账，分类账

journal entry
分录，流水分录

journalize
分录

journal voucher
分录凭单

journeyman
伙计，短工

judgment
审判，裁决

judgment creditor
胜诉债权人

judgment debtor
败诉债务人

judgment lien
判决留置权

judgment proof
无能力还债者

judgment sample
审计决定

judicial bond
司法保证

judicial foreclosure or judicial sale
司法没收或法院判决的拍卖

jumbo certificate of deposit
巨额存款证明

junior issue
后序发行，低级证券

junior lien
低级留置权

junior mortgage
低级抵押权

junior partner
低级合伙人

junior security
次级证券

junk bond
垃圾债券

jurisdiction
管辖权，司法权

jurisprudence
裁决，国际裁决

jury
陪审团

just compensation
正当补偿，合理补偿

justifiable
公正的，合理的

justified price
合理价格

K

Keogh plan
吉奥老年金计划

key (c)
键，关键字，密钥

key-area evaluation
关键领域评估理论

keyboard (c)
键盘

**key person life and
health insurance**
企业主管人员人寿及健康
保险

kickback
回扣，佣金

kicker
附加好处

kiddie tax
儿童税务责任

killing
赚大钱，大发利市

kiting
开空头支票，挪用

know-how
专有技术，诀窍

knowledge intensive
知识密集型

**know-your-customer
rule**
了解客户需要规则

kudos
奖赏，赞扬

L

labeling laws
标签法
labor
劳工，人力，工人
labor agreement
劳资协议
labor dispute
劳资纠纷
labor force
劳动力
labor intensive
劳动密集型
labor mobility
劳力流动性
labor piracy
引诱工人跳槽，挖角
labor pool
劳动人口库
labor union
工会，工人联合会
laches
因延误而丧失履行合约的权
利
lading
装载，装船
lagging indicator
滞后指标
LAN
(local area network) (c)
lan（局域网）

land
地产，土地
land banking
购买准备将来使用的土地
land contract
土地合约
land development
土地开发
landlocked
内陆土地，内陆国
landlord
地主
landmark
界标
landscape
(format) (c)
横向（格式）
land trust
土地信托
land-use intensity
土地使用密度
land-use planning
土地使用规划
land-use regulation
土地使用规定
land-use succession
土地使用继承
lapping
挪后补前，截留，
移用

lapse
过期失效，作废，终止
lapsing schedule
固定资产增减明细表
last in, first out (LIFO)
后进先出（LIFO）
last sale
最近销售，当天收盘价
latent defect
潜在缺陷
latitude
活动余地
law
法律，法令，规律，法则
law of diminishing returns
报酬递减律
law of increasing costs
成本递增法则
law of large numbers
大数法则
law of supply and demand
供求法则
lay off
解雇，暂时停业
leader
领导者，大户，特价品，先
导指数
leader pricing
特价品定价政策
leading indicators
主要指标
lead time
生产准备时间，订货至交货
时间
lease
租约，租赁

leasehold
租赁物，租借期，租约
leasehold improvement
租赁物改良
leasehold insurance
租赁物保险
leasehold mortgage
租借抵押
leasehold value
租借价值
lease with option to purchase
有权购买的租赁
least-effort principle
最省力原则
leave of absence
获准假期
ledger
分类账，明细账
legal entity
合法组织，法定单位
legal investment
合法投资
legal list
合法证券
legal monopoly
合法垄断
legal name
依法登记的名称
legal notice
法律通知
legal opinion
法律意见，律师意见，
法律说明
legal right
合法权利

legal tender
法定货币

legal wrong
侵权

legatee
遗嘱接受人

lender
出借人，出租人，放款人，
债权人

lessee
承租人，承租方，
租户

lessor
出租人，出租方

less than carload (L/C)
零担货运（L/C）

letter of intent
意向书

letter stock
非注册股票

level debt service
均衡还债

level out
平衡，稳定

level-payment income stream
平衡支付收入流

level-payment mortgage
平衡支付抵押贷款

level premium
平均保险费

leverage
杠杆作用，借贷机会，浮动
股息

leveraged buyout (LBO)
融资买断

leveraged company
负债较高的公司

leveraged lease
融资租赁

levy
征税，征集，征税额，
扣押

liability
负债，义务，债务

liability, business exposures
商业风险责任

liability, civil
民事责任

liability, criminal
刑事责任

liability dividend
负债股利

liability insurance
责任保险

liability, legal
法律责任

liability, professional
职业责任

liable
应负责任

libel
诽谤，侮辱，
中伤

license
许可证，特许证，认可，
授权

license bond
许可保证金

licensee
买方，受证人，
被许可人

license law
执业法，
牌照法
licensing examination
执照考试
lien
留置权，扣押权
life cycle
寿命周期，耐用年数
life estate
终身产业
life expectancy
平均寿命，
预期使用期限
life tenant
终身受益人
lighterage
驳船费
like-kind property
同类财产
limited audit
有限审计
limited company
有限公司
limited distribution
限额分配
limited liability
有限责任
limited occupancy agreement
有限占用协议
limited or special partner
有限或特殊合伙人
limited partnership
有限合伙企业

limited payment life insurance
限期交费终身保单
limit order
限价定单，限制性定单
limit up, limit down
升达限幅，降至限幅
line
生产线，航线，行业，生意，种类，限度
line and staff organization
条块式组织结构
line authority
生产线主管
line control
生产控制，组织控制
line extension
产品扩展
line function
生产功能
line management
生产线管理，直线管理
line of credit
信用额度
line organization
生产组织
line pitch (c)
线间距
line printer
行式打印机
link (c)
链接，链路
linked object (c)
链接对象
liquid asset
流动资产

liquidate
清算，变线，平仓
liquidated damages
清偿损失额，
赔偿金
liquidated debt
已清算债务额
liquidated value
已清算价值
liquidation
清盘，清算，结清，变现，
清理
liquidation dividend
清算分摊额
**liquid crystal display
(LCD)**
液晶显示器
liquidity
周转率，流动性，
变现能力
liquidity preference
流动偏好
liquidity ratio
现金周转率，清算比率
list
一览表，价目表，清单，
名单
listed options
上市期权
listed security
上市证券
listing
上市，挂牌
**listing agent, listing
broker**
上市代理，上市经纪人

listing requirements
上市要求
list price
价目表价格，批发价
litigant
诉讼
litigation
诉讼，争论
living trust
生前信托，有效信托
load
装船，加载，加收额外费用
load fund
加收交易费的互助基金
loan
贷款，借款
loan application
贷款申请书
loan committee
贷款委员会
loan-to-value ratio (LTV)
借款价值比率（LTV）
loan value
借款价值
lobbyist
院外活动集团成员
lock box
银行存款箱
locked in
被锁住，锁定，套牢
lockout
封闭工厂
lock-up option
封存选择权
log in (log on) (c)
注册（登录）

login identification
(login ID) (c)
注册标识
（注册 id）

logic diagram (c)
逻辑图

logo
徽标，标志

log off (c)
注销

long bond
长期债券

long coupon
长期息票

longevity pay
按资历增加的工资

long position
进远期货，多头，买超，
多头市场

long-range planning
远景规划

long-term debt or long-term
liability
长期债务或长期负债

long-term gain (loss)
长期收益（损失）

long-term trend
长期趋势

long-wave cycle
长周期

loop
环，环路，循环

loophole
漏洞

loose rein
放松型管理

loss
损失，亏损，错过

loss adjustment expense
理算费用

loss carryback
回计亏损

loss carryforward
计入后期亏损

loss contingency
或有损失

loss leader
亏本出售，特廉商品

loss of income insurance
收入损失保险

loss ratio
损失率，赔款率

lot and block
分块土地定位法

lot line
地块边界线

lottery
彩票

low
证券最低价

lower case
character/letter (c)
小写字符/字母

lower-involvement
model
低参与模型

lower of cost or market
以成本或市价低者为准

low-grade
低等，次品

low resolution (c)
低分辨率

low-tech
低技术产品

lump sum
总价，总计，总数

lumpsum distribution
一次性总付

lump-sum purchase
整套购买，整批购买

luxury tax
奢侈品税

M

macro (c)
宏(功能，指令)

macroeconomics
宏观经济学

macroenvironment
宏观环境

magnetic card (c)
磁卡

magnetic strip
磁条

mailbox (c)
信箱区，邮箱

mail fraud
邮寄诈骗

mailing list
邮寄清单

mainframe (c)
大型计算机；主机；
主机柜；底盘

main menu (c)
主选项屏[菜单，
选单]

maintenance
维护，维修

maintenance bond
维修契约，
维修保证

maintenance fee
维修费，维持费

maintenance method
维修期

majority
多数

majority shareholder
多数股持有人

maker
制造商，出票人，制单人

make-work
无价值工作

malicious mischief
恶意伤害

malingerer
装病逃差的人

malingering
装病，开小差

mall
封闭式购物中心

malpractice
渎职，违法行为

manage
管理，经营

managed account
管理账户，经营账户

managed currency
管理货币，管理通货

managed economy
管制经济，计划经济

management
管理，主管，管理当局

management agreement
管理协议

management audit
经营审计

management by crisis
危机管理

management by exception
例外事件管理

management by objective
(MBO)
目标管理（MBO）

management by walking
around (MBWA)
注重人际交流的管理方法
（MBWA）

management consultant
经营顾问，业务顾问

management cycle
管理循环

management fee
管理费

management game
管理训练

management guide
管理指导手册

management information
system (MIS)
管理信息系统（MIS）

management
prerogative
管理特权

management ratio
管理人员比例

management science
管理科学

management style
管理风格

management system
管理系统

manager
经理

managerial accounting
管理会计

managerial grid
管理人员领导行为分类方
法

mandate
授权书，委托书，委托

mandatory copy
命令副本

man-hour
人时

manifest
舱单，装货单，声明

manipulation
操纵，篡改，控制，操作，
处理

manual
手册，指南，
手工操作的

manual skill
手工技巧

manufacture
制造商，厂家

manufacturing cost
制造成本

manufacturing
inventory
生产库存

manufacturing order
生产指令，制造任务书

map
地图，示意图

margin
保证金，价差，
边缘，余额，押金，
毛利

margin account
保证金账户，
边际账户

marginal cost
边际成本

marginal cost curve
边际成本区线

marginal efficiency of capital
资本边际效率

marginal producer
边际生产者

marginal propensity to consume (MPC)
边际消费倾向（MPC）

marginal propensity to invest
边际投资倾向

marginal propensity to save (MPS)
边际储蓄倾向
（MPS）

marginal property
边际财产

marginal revenue
边际收入

marginal tax rate
边际税率

marginal utility
边际效用

margin call
交纳保证金通知

margin of profit
利润边际

margin of safety
安全边际

margins
保证金，价差，边缘，
余额，押金

marital deduction
配偶扣除

markdown
减价，降价

market
市场，市价，商业中心，
销售，推销

marketablility
可销性，适销性

marketable securities
有价证券，可转让政权

marketable title
适销证券，可转让产权

market aggregation
市场统合，统一市场

market analysis
市场分析

market area
市场区域

market basket
市场指标性商品组合

market comparison approach
市场比较法

market demand
市场需求

market development index
市场发展指数

market economy
市场经济

market equilibrium
市场供需平衡

market index
市价指数

marketing
营销，市场销售

marketing concept
营销观点，
市场学概念

marketing director
市场部经理

marketing information system
市场营销信息系统

marketing mix
营销组合

marketing plan
营销计划

marketing research
市场研究

market letter
市场简报，行情通报

market order
市场指令

market penetration
市场渗透

market price
市价，时价，市场价格

market rent
市面租金

market research
市场调查

market segmentation
区隔市场

market share
市场份额占有率

market system
市场体制，销售系统

market test
市场试验

market timing
营销时机

market value
市场价值

market value clause
市场价值条款

mark to the market
逐日盯市

markup
加价，加利

marriage penalty
婚姻税务加重

marxism
马克思主义

mask (c)
掩模，掩码，
屏蔽

mass appeal
集体诉讼

mass communication
大众广告

mass media
大众媒体

mass production
大批量生产

master boot record (c)
主引导记录

master lease
主租约

master limited partnership
主要有限合伙企业

master plan
主要计划，主规划图，总体计划

master policy
主保险单，总保单

master-servant rule
主仆规则

masthead
桅顶，旗杆之顶

matching principle
收支对应原则

material
原料，材料，物资，实质性的

material fact
重要事实

materiality
物质性，重要性，实质性

material man
建材供应商

materials handling
原料管理，材料搬运

materials management
物料管理，物资管理

matrix
矩阵，真值表

matrix organization
矩阵式组织结构

matured endowment
到期证券或保险金

mature economy
成熟经济

maturity
到期，偿还日，期限

maturity date
到期日

maximize (c)
最大化

maximum capacity
最大产能

M-CATS
市政应计证券证明

mean, arithmetic
算数平均值

mean, geometric
几何平均值

mean return
平均回报

mechanic's lien
技工留置权

mechanization
机械化

media
媒体，媒介

media buy
广告时段购买

media buyer
广告时段购买人

media option
广告手段选择

media plan
广告手段计划者

media planner
仲裁，调解

media player (c)
媒体播放器

mediation
广告影响度

media weight
医疗检查

medical examination
医疗检查

medium
中等，媒介，工具

medium of exchange
交换媒介

medium-term bond
中期债券

meeting of the minds
合同条款经由各方同意

megabucks
百万美元

megabyte
兆字节

member bank
会员银行

member firm or member corporation
会员公司

memorandum
备忘录，纪要，摘要，通知单

memory
记忆，记录，存储，
(c) 存储器，内存

menial
卑下的，不体面的工作

menu bar (c)
选项栏[条，区，行]

mercantile
商业的

mercantile agency
商业征信所

mercantile law
商法

mercantilism
重商主义，商业习惯

merchandise
商品，经商，推销

merchandise allowance
商品折扣

merchandise broker
商品经纪人

merchandise control
商品控制

merchandising
商品学，商品销售

merchandising director
商品销售主管

merchandising service
商品服务

merchantable
有销路的，
可销售的

merchant bank
商业银行

merge
合并

merger
合并，兼并

merit increase
功绩报酬上涨

merit rating
等级税率

meter rate
电表计费率

metes and bounds
地产边界

methods-time
measurement (MTM)
时间计量方法（MTM）

metrication
公制，米制

metric system
公制，十进位制

metropolitan area
大都会区

microeconomics
微观经济学

micromotion study
微动研究

midcareer plateau
职业升迁障碍

middle management
中级管理层

midnight deadline
零时截止时间

migrate (c)
迁移

migratory worker
流动工人

military-industrial
complex
军队-企业关系

milking
利用局势谋取私利

milking strategy
操纵市场从中谋利

millage rate
按英里里程计算运费率

millionaire
百万富翁

millionaire on paper
名义百万富翁

mineral rights
采矿权

minimax principle
极大极小原则

minimize (c)
最小化

minimum lease payments
最低租金

minimum lot area
最小地段面积

minimum pension liability
最低养老金责任

minimum permium
deposit plan
最低保险费储蓄计划

minimum wage
最低工资

minor
未成年人

minority interest or
minority investment
少数权益或少数投资

mintage
造币，铸币权，硬币

minutes
会议记录

misdemeanor
不端行为

mismanagement
管理不善

misrepresentation
错误报道，歪曲

misstatement of age
慌报年龄

mistake
错误

mistake of law
引用法律不当
mitigation of damages
减轻损失，减少损害费
mix
组合，组成，结构，混合
mixed economy
混合经济
mixed perils
混合危险
mixed signals
混乱信息
mode
模式，方式，样式，时尚，状况
modeling
模拟，模型化，成型
modeling language
模型化语言，模拟语言
model unit
样板单位
modern portfolio theory (MPT)
现代投资组合理论（MPT）
modified accrual
修正权责会计法
modified life insurance
修正人寿保险
modified union shop
重建的全工会成员工厂
module (c)
模块，组件
mom and pop store
小零售商店

momentum
价格变动速度，势力，力量
monetarist
货币学派
monetary
货币的，金融的
monetary item
货币项目，金融项目
monetary reserve
货币储备
monetary standard
货币本位
money
钱，现金，货币，款项
money illusion
货币幻觉
money income
货币收入，现金收入
money market
金融市场，货币市场
money market fund
用在短期资金市场投资的资金
money supply
货币供应量，货币发行量
monopolist
垄断者，独占的
monopoly
垄断
monopoly price
垄断价格
monopsony
买主垄断，统购，专买

monthly compounding of interest
按月复计利息

monthly investment plan
按月投资计划

month-to-month tenancy
按月租赁

monument
界标，界石

moonlighting
兼职工作

morale
士气，道德

moral hazard
品行危险

moral law
道德准则

moral obligation bond
义务债券

moral suasion
道德劝告

moratorium
延期偿付，延缓履行

mortality table
死亡统计表

mortgage
典当，抵押，抵押权

mortgage assumption
抵押责任

mortgage-backed certificate
抵押权证书

mortgage-backed security
抵押证券

mortgage banker
经营抵押业务的银行家

mortgage bond
抵押债券

mortgage broker
抵押经纪人

mortgage commitment
抵押承诺

mortgage constant
抵押常数

mortgage correspondent
收费抵押服务经纪人

mortgage debt
抵押债务

mortgage discount
抵押折扣

mortgagee
承受抵押者，受抵押人

mortgage insurance
抵押保险

mortgage insurance policy
抵押保险单

mortgage lien
抵押留置权

mortgage out
超额抵押融资

mortgage relief
抵押解除

mortgage servicing
抵押管理

mortgagor
抵押人

motion study
动作研究

motivation
动机，动力，促动因素，激励

motor freight
汽车运费

mouse (c)
鼠标器

mouse pad (c)
鼠标垫

movement
价格变动

mover and shaker
具有超常影响力的人

moving average
移动平均数,
移动均值

muckraker
政商腐败揭露者

multibuyer
多次购买者

multicasting (c)
多投影，多映射

multicollinearity
多边共线性

multiemployer bargaining
多雇主谈判

multifunction (c)
多功能

multimedia
多媒体

multinational corporation (MNC)
跨国公司（MNC）

multiple
多种，复合

multiple listing
多家房产公司信息登记

multiple locations forms
多址财产保险单

multiple-management plan
多方参加管理计划

multiple-peril insurance
多种风险保险

multiple regression
复合回归分析

multiple retirement ages
复合退休年龄

multiple shop
联号商店

multiplier
乘数

multiuser (c)
多用户

municipal bond
市政公债

municipal revenue bond
市政收入债券

muniments of title
产权契据

mutual association
互助储蓄贷款协会

mutual company
合股公司

mutual fund
互助基金，共同基金

mutual insurance company
相互保险公司

mutuality of contract
合同双方关系

N

naked option
无保证期权

naked position
无担保部位

named peril policy
指定危险保险单

name position bond
记名职位忠诚保险

name schedule bond
在册雇员忠诚保险

nationalization
国有化

national wealth
国民财富

natural business year
自然营业年度

natural monopoly
自然垄断

natural resources
自然资源

navigation (c)
导航

near money
类货币，准货币

need satisfaction
需要得到满足

negative amortization
负摊还

negative carry
账面赔本

negative cash flow
负现金流量

negative correlation
负相关

negative income tax
负所得税

negative working capital
负周转资金，负运用资本

negligence
疏忽

negotiable
可议付的，可转让的

negotiable certificate of
deposit
可转让存款单

negotiable instrument
可转让票据

negotiable order of
withdrawl (NOW)
能开可转让支付命令的活
期存款账户 (NOW)

negotiated market
price
议价市场价格

negotiated price
议付价

negotiation
谈判，协商，议付

neighborhood store
社区商店

neoclassical economics
新古典经济学

nepotism
任人唯亲

nest egg
储备金

net
纯净，净价，净额，净得

net assets
净资产

net asset value (NAV)
资产净值（NAV）

net book value
账面净值

net contribution
净贡献额

net cost
净价，实价，
净成本

net current assets
净流动资产

net income
净收入

net income per share of common stock
普通股每股净收入

net leasable area
可租赁净面积

net lease
纯租赁

net listing
净标价

net loss
损失净额

net national product
国民生产净值

net operating income (NOI)
营业净收益（NOI）

net operating loss (NOL)
营业净损失（NOL）

net present value (NPV)
净现值（NPV）

net proceeds
净收入，实得额

net profit
净利，纯利润

net profit margin
纯利润率，净利率

net purchases
购货净额

net quick assets
速动资产净额

net rate
净比例，净费率

net realizable value
可变现净值

net sales
净销售额

net surfing (c)
网上浏览

net transaction
净交易

network (c)
网络

network administrator (c)
网络管理员

networking
联网

net yield
净收益，净产量

new issue
股票等的初次上市发行

new money
新货币

newspaper syndicate
新闻联合组织

new town
新城镇

niche
恰当的地方，活动范围

night letter
夜间书信电报

node (c)
节点，结点

no-growth
无增长

no-load fund
无负担基金

nominal account
名义账户

nominal damages
象征性损失

nominal interest rate
名义利率，虚利率

nominal scale
名义规模

nominal wage
名义工资

nominal yield
名义收益

nominee
被提名人

noncallable
到期偿还优先股票或债券

noncompetitive bid
非竞争性招标

nonconforming use
不符合规定的土地使用

noncontestability clause
无争议性条款

noncumulative preferred stock
非累积优先股

noncurrent asset
非流动资产

nondeductibility of employer contributions
不可扣除性雇主贡献额

nondiscretionary trust
非自主信托

nondisturbance clause
非变动条款

nondurable goods
非耐用品

nonformatted (c)
非格式化的

nonglare (c)
不闪光的

nonmember bank
非会员银行

nonmember firm
非会员公司

nonmonetary item
非货币性项目

nonnegotiable instrument
不可转让票据

nonoperating expense (revenue)
非营业费用（收入）

nonparametric statistics
非参数统计

nonperformance
不履行，不清偿
nonproductive
非生产性的
nonproductive loan
非生产性贷款
nonprofit accounting
非营利会计
nonprofit corporation
非营利性公司
nonpublic information
不公开资料
nonrecourse
无追索权
nonrecurring charge
临时性费用
nonrefundable
不退款的
nonrefundable fee or nonrefundable deposit
不退还的收费或不退还的定金
nonrenewable natural resources
不能再生的能源
nonstock corporation
非股份公司
nonstore retailing
无商品销售
nonvoting stock
无投票选举权的股票
no-par stock
无面额股票
norm
定额，标准，典型

normal price
正常价格，标准价格
normal profit
正常利润
normal retirement age
正常退休年龄
normal wear and tear
正常损耗
normative economics
规范经济学
no-strike clause
不罢工条款
notarize
公证
note
纸币，票据，借据，注释，照会
notebook computer (c)
笔记本式计算机
note payable
应付票据
note receivable
应收票据
not for profit
非营利
notice
通知书，布告，注意
notice of cancellation clause
撤销通知条款
notice of default
违约通知
notice to quit
解雇通知
not rated (NR)
未评级（NR）

novation

更新，代替

NSF

存款不足

nuisance

小额，低税

null and void

无效，作废

num lock key (c)

数字锁定键

O

objective
目标，客观的

objective value
客观价值

obligation bond
责任债券

obligee
权利人，债权人

obligor
义务人，债务人

observation test
观察测验

obsolescence
废弃

occupancy level
租出率

occupancy, occupant
占有，居住

occupation
占用，职业，开业

occupational analysis
职业分析

occupational disease
职业病

occupational group
职业类别

occupational hazard
职业危险

odd lot
零星股票，零星交易

odd page (c)
奇数页

odd-value pricing
临时计价，奇零定价法

offer
发盘，出价，报价，提供，
给予，要约

offer and acceptance
报盘及接受

offeree
接盘人，受盘人

offerer
发盘人，报价人

offering date
报价日期

offering price
报出价格

office management
办公室管理

official exchange rate
法定汇率，官方汇率

off-line
脱机

off peak
非高峰

off-price
低价

off-sale date
从货架撤下日期

offset
抵消，冲销，对冲，补偿，平仓

offshore
近岸，境外

off-site cost
间接成本，间接费用

off the balance sheet
未在资产负债表中列出的交易

off the books
账外

off time
非服务时间，时间外

oil and gas lease
油气租赁

oligopoly
卖主寡头垄断

ombudsman
巡查官，机构内负责听取意见的人

omitted dividend
略去的分红

on account
赊账，记账

onboard computer
机载计算机

on demand
即期，见票即付

one-cent sale
名义出售，白送

one-hundred-percent location
销售额最高的店面

one-minute manager
过分简单化的经理

one-time buyer
一次性购买者

one-time rate
一次性费率

on-line (c)
线上，在线，联机

on-line data base
在线数据库

on order
已订货物，在订购中

on-sale date
上市日

on speculation (on spec)
投机活动（ON SPEC）

on-the-job training (OJT)
在职培训（OJT）

open
未结清的，自由开放的，公开的，开信用证

open account
未清账户，往来账户

open bid
公开招标

open dating
注明期限

open distribution
开发式分销

open-door policy
门户开放政策

open economy
开放经济

open-end
开放，开口，公开

open-end lease
开口租赁

open-end management
company
开放式管理公司

open-end mortgage
开放抵押

open house
公开展示

open housing
开放房屋

opening
开业，开盘，出售，开始，机会，开放

open interest
未结清权益，空盘量

open listing
公开地产代理权

open-market rates
公开市场汇率

open mortgage
可加抵押

open order
开口定单，未完成定单

open outcry
公开喊价

open shop
开放制工厂或商店

open space
开放空间

open stock
期初存款，期初存货

open-to-buy
可购限额，准购定额

open union
开放式工会

operand
操作数，基数

operating cycle
营业周期，经营周期

operating expense
营业费用，使用费

operating lease
经营性租赁，营业租赁

operating loss
营业亏损，经营亏损

operating profit (loss)
营业利润（损失）

operating ratio
开工率，经营比率

operating system
操作系统

operational audit
业务审计，营业核查

operational control
营业管理

operation mode (c)
操作模式

operations research (OR)
运筹学习 (OR)

operator (c)
运算符，操作员，操作

opinion
意见

opinion leader
意见领导人

opinion of title
产权意见

opportunity cost
机会成本

optical character
recognition
(OCR) (c)
光学字符识别 （OCR）

optical fiber (c)
光导纤维，光纤

optimum capacity
最适生产能力

option
期权，选择权，约束力，优先购买权

optional modes of settlement
人寿险赔偿方式选择

option holder
选择权持有人

oral contract
口头协议

orange goods
橙类消费物品

or better
或者更好价格

order
秩序，订货，定单，抬头人，汇票，指示

order bill of lading
指定人提单

order card
订购卡

order entry
定单内容记录

order flow pattern
定单流动模式

order form
定货单，定单格式

order number
定单编号

order paper
指示票据，记名票据

order-point system
定货点系统

order regulation
定货规定

ordinal scale
顺序量表

ordinance
法令，条例，法规，布告

ordinary and necessary business expense
普通及必要的商业开支

ordinary annuity
普通年金

ordinary course of business
正常业务程序

ordinary gain or ordinary income
正常收益或收入

ordinary interest
正常利息

ordinary loss
正常损失

ordinary payroll exclusion endorsement
正常工资单免列认可

organization
组织，机构，体制，编制，建制，机关

organizational behavior
组织行为

organizational chart
组织机构图

organization cost
开办成本，组织费用

organization development
组织改进

organization planning
组织计划

organization structure
组织结构

organized labor
有组织的劳动力

orientation
定向，方向性

original cost
原始成本，最初成本

original entry
原始记入账

original issue discount (OID)
原始发行股票折扣（OID）

original maturity
原定偿还期

original order
原定单

origination fee
开办费

originator
创始人，原始承销人

other income
其它收入

other insurance clause
其它保险条款

other people's money
借入款

outbid
抬高出价

outcry market
喊价成交，拍卖市场

outline view (c)
大纲视图

out of the money
认购价格

outlet store
代销店

outside director
外部董事，不参与管理的董事

outsourcing
外协

outstanding
应付未付，未清

outstanding balance
未付差额

outstanding capital stock
净发股本

overage
超额，超过部分，溢数

overall expenses method
总费用方法

overall rate of return
总回报率

over-and-short
溢缺

overbooked
订座超出

overbought
多头，买空，超买

overcharge
收费过多
overflow
超溢
overhang
悬置
overhead
制造费用，间接费用
overheating
过热
overimprovement
改善过度
overissue
溢发，超额发行
overkill
过度推销
overpayment
多付，超付
overproduction
生产过剩
override
代理佣金

overrun
超过，超出
over (short)
超出（短缺）
over the counter (OTC)
直接交易（OTC）
over-the-counter retailing
直接零售
overtime
加班，超时
overtrading
超额经营
overvalued
计值过高的
overwrite (c)
重写，覆写
owner-operator
物主-操作人
ownership
所有权
ownership form
所有权形式

P

pacesetter
模范，标兵

package
统包价格，整批，
一揽子

package band
包装条广告

package code
包装代码

package design
包装设计

packaged goods
包装货物

package mortgage
一揽子抵押贷款

packing list
包装物详单，
装箱单

padding
填料，虚报账目

page break (c)
分页符

page down (c)
页下移，版面往下移

page format (c)
页格式

page up (c)
页上移，
版面往上移

pagination (c)
标页码，分页

paid in advance
已提前支付

paid-in capital
实收资本，缴入资本

paid-in surplus
缴入盈余，盈余

paid status
支付情况

paintbrush (c)
画笔

painting the tape
托市

palmtop (c)
掌上型

paper
钞票，纸币，票据，
证券，汇票，支票

paper gold
纸黄金

paper jam (c)
卡纸

paper money
纸币，钞票，票据，
支票

paper profit
(loss)
账面利润（损失）

par
面额，平价，同等地位，
平均的

paralegal
律师的专职助手

parallel connection (c)
并联连接

parallel processing
平行处理

parameter
参数，数据

par bond
平价债券

parcel
包裹，邮包

parent company
母公司，总公司

parity
平价，比价

parity check
奇偶校验

parity price
平价，对等价格

parking
安全投资

parliament procedure
正式程序

partial delivery
部分交货，局部交割

partial-equilibrium analysis
部分均衡分析

partial release
部分解除索赔权

partial taking
部分获得

participating insurance
参与保险，分享保险

participating policy
分享保单

participating preferred stock
共享优先股

participation certificate
参与权益证书

participation loan
参与贷款，共同

participative budgeting
职工参与型预算制

participative leadership
参与型领导方法

partition
划分，分割，分配

partner
合伙人，合伙董事

partnership
合伙关系，合伙企业，
合股

part-time
兼任

par value
票面价值

passed dividend
过期未付的股息

passenger mile
旅客里程

passive activities
被动管理

passive income (loss)
被动收入（损失）

passive investor
被动投资人

passport
护照

pass-through security
转嫁证券

password
通行口令，密码

paste (c)
粘贴

past service benefit
过去服务年资收益

patent
专利，专利权

patent infringement
侵犯专利权

patent monopoly
专利独占

patent of invention
发明专利

patent pending
专利申请

patent warfare
专利战

paternalism
家长式作风，
温和的干涉主义

path (c)
路径，通路

patronage dividend and rebate
赞助人红利及回扣

pauper
穷人，乞丐

pay
支付，付款，偿还，工资

payables
应付款

pay as you go
分期付款，按成收费

payback period
偿付期

paycheck
工资支票

payday
发薪日，结算日

payee
受款人，收款人

payer
付款人

paying agent
代付人

payload
工资负担，付运费的货物

payment bond
付款债券

payment date
付款日期

payment in due course
期满兑付

payment method
支付方法，付款方法

payola
贿赂，收买

payout
偿付，补偿

payout ratio
股息支付率，股利发放率

pay period
工资支付期，工资结算期

payroll
工资单

payroll deduction
工薪扣款

payroll savings plan
工资储蓄计划

payroll tax
工薪税

peak
最高，高峰

peak period
高峰期间

peculation
盗用公款

pecuniary
金钱的

peg
固定

penalty
罚款

penny stock
便士股票，低价股票

pension fund
抚恤基金，退休基金

peon
日工，散工

people intensive
人工密集型

per capita
人均

per-capita debt
人均负债

percentage lease
分成租约

percentage-of-completion method
按完成进度报税法

percentage-of-sales method
销售百分比法

percent, percentage
百分比

percolation test
渗透测试

per diem
每日津贴

perfect competition
完全竞争

perfect (pure) monopoly
完全垄断

perfected
完美的

performance
履行，完成，业绩，表现，清偿

performance bond
履约保证金

performance fund
营业基金

performance stock
绩优股

period
会计期，时期，周期，有效期

period expense, period cost
期间费用，期间成本

periodic inventory method
定期盘存法

peripheral device (c)
外围设备，外部设备

perishable perjury
易损伪证

permanent difference
恒差，永久差别

permanent financing
长期融资，长期抵押贷款

permit
许可证，执照，许可

permit bond
许可证押金

permutations
变更，交换，彻底改变

perpetual inventory
永续盘存

perpetuity
永久，永久财产，终身年金

perquisite (perk)
津贴，奖金，额外收入

person
人，本人，法人

personal data sheet
个人资料

personal digital assistant (PDA) (c)
个人数字助理（PDA）

personal financial statement
个人财务报表

personal holding company (phc)
个人持股公司（PHC）

personal income
个人收入

personal influence
个人影响

personal injury
个人伤害

personal liability
个人责任

personal property
个人财产

personal property floater
私人财产总括

personal selling
个人推销

personnel
人员，人事

personnel department
人事部门

petition
请求，请求书

petty cash fund
零用现金基金

Phillip's curve
菲利浦斯曲线

physical commodity
实物商品

physical depreciation
实际折旧，实物折旧，有形损耗

physical examination
实物检查

physical inventory
实地盘存

picketing
站在公共建筑物前表示抗议的示威群众

picture format (c)
图片格式

piece rate
计件工资，论件计

piece work
计件工作

pie chart
圆形分析图

pie chart/graph (c)
饼形图

pier to house
码头到仓库运输

piggyback loan
寄生贷款

pilot plan
新产品试制计划

pin money
零用钱

pipeline
管道

pitch (c)
孔距，间距，声调

pixel/picture element (c)
象素/象元

pixel image (c)
象素映象

placement test
招工测试

place utility
商品摆放效应

plain text (c)
明文；纯文本

plaintiff
原告

plan
计划，规划，方案，方法，
制度

plan b
备用计划

planned economy
计划经济

plant
工厂，车间，设备，
固定资产

plat
绘制土地图，规划

plat book
土地使用图

pleading
抗辩，承认

pledge
典当，抵押，抵押权

plot
地块，图谋，绘图

plot plan
土地使用规划

plottage value
地块整合价值

plotter
绘图机

plow back
再投资

plus tick
证券价格上涨符号

pocket computer (c)
袖珍型计算机

point
地点，细目，条款

point chart (c)
点图，散点图

poison pill
毒丸计划

poisson distribution
泊松分布

police power
警察权力

policy holder
保险客户，投保人

policy loan
保险单贷款

pollution
污染

pool
集合基金，联营

pooling of interests
合并经营，利益共享

portal-to-portal pay
门对门旅费全包

portfolio
业务责任，有价证券，资财，投资搭配

portfolio beta score
有价证券贝塔值

portfolio income
证券收入

portfolio manger
有价证券管理人

portfolio reinsurance
有价证券再保险

portfolio theory
投资搭配理论

port of entry
进口港

portrait (format) (c)
纵向（格式）

position
位置，金融头寸，期货进货，额度

positioning
定位

positive confirmation
正向确认

positive leverage
正借贷投资收益

positive yield curve
正产出曲线

possession
保有，拥有

post closing trial balance
结账后试算表

posting
过账，(c) 贴出，显出，记入

poverty
贫困

power connection (c)
电源连接

power down (c)
电源关闭，掉电

power of attorney
委托书，律师代理权

power of sale
销售权

power surge
权力高峰

power up (c)
加电

practical capacity
实际生产能力

pre-bill
事前账单

precautionary motive
预防动机

preclosing
结账前

precompute
预先计算

prediction
预测，推测

preemptive rights
优先认购权

preexisting use
已存在使用权

prefabricated
预制的

preferential rehiring
优先再雇用

preferred dividend
优先股息

preferred dividend coverage
优先股总收入

preferred stock
优先股

prelease
预租赁

preliminary prospectus
初步募股书

premises
前序

premium
保险费，溢价，奖金

premium bond
有奖公债，溢价债券

premium income
保险费收入

premium pay
加班费，奖金

premium rate
保险费率

prenuptial agreement
婚前协议

prepaid
已预付，先付的

prepaid expense
预付费用

prepaid-interest
预付利息

prepayment
预付，先付

prepayment clause
预付条款

prepayment penalty
提前偿付罚金

prepayment privilege
预付权利

prerogative
特权，君权

presale
预售

prescription
规定，时效，处方

presentation
交兑，议付

present fairly
现时公平资料

present value
现值

present value of 1
一元现值

present value of annuity
年金现值

president
总裁，总经理，会长，
行长

presold issue
预售一空的政府债券

press kit
公司就某一事件向媒体发放
的信息资料

prestige advertising
形象提升广告

prestige pricing
威信性高价策略

pretax earnings
税前收入

pretax rate of return
税前回报率

preventive maintenance
预防性维护
price elasticity
价格弹性
price-fixing
价格管制，定价，限价，
价格垄断
price index
价格指数
price lining
底价
price stabilization
稳定物价
price support
价格补贴
price system
价格制度，价格体制
price war
价格战
pricey
昂贵的，高价的，
价格离谱的
pricing below market
低于市场价格的定价政策
primary boycott
一级抵制，初级抵制
primary demand
初级需求
primary distribution
股票或债券初次上市发行，
初次分配
primary earnings per (common) share
基本每股（普通股）收益
primary lease
主要租赁

primary market
初级市场，原始市场，
主要市场
primary market area
报纸目标发行区，
主要销售区
primary package
主包装
prime paper
最佳票据，无风险票据
prime rate
基本贷款利率，优惠利率
prime tenant
主要租户
principal
主要的，本金的
principal amount
本金
principal and interest payment (P&I)
本息付款（P&I）
principal, interest, taxes, and insurance payment (PITI)
本金，利息，税务，保险支付（PITI）
principal residence
主要居住地
principal stock holder
主要持股人
principal sum
本金，本金额
printer (c)
打印机
printout (c)
打印输出，印出

prior period
adjustment
上期调整

prior-preferred stock
最优先股

prior service cost
前期服务成本

privacy laws
隐私法

private cost
私人开支

private limited
partnership
私营有限公司

private mortgage
insurance
私营抵押保险

private offering or
private placement
不公开出售或直接销售

privatization
私有化

privity
当事人关系

prize broker
以奖品换广告经纪人

probate
遗嘱检验，检验

probationary employee
试用期雇员，
记过雇员

proceeds
进行，前往，收益，
收入

proceeds from resale
重售收益

processor upgrade (c)
处理器升级

procurement
采购，获得，
供货合同

procurring cause
成事归因

produce
生产，产物，
产生

producer cooperative
厂商合作组织

producer goods
生产资料，生产物资，
机器设备

product
产品，产物，成果

production
生产，产品，制造品

production control
生产控制，生产管理

production-oriented
organization
以生产为主的企业

production-possibility
curve
生产—可能性曲线

production rate
生产率

production worker
生产工人

productivity
生产率，生产能力，
多产

product liability
产品责任

product liability insurance
产品责任保险

product life cycle
产品寿命周期

product line
生产线，产品系列

product mix
产品结构，产品搭配

profession
专门职业，专业，工种

profit
赢利，利润，收入

profitability
有利性，赢利性，获利能力

profit and loss statemnt (P&L)
损益表（P&L）

profit center
利润中心，盈利部门

profiteer
贪图暴利者，奸商

profit margin
利润边际

profit motive
利润动机

profits and commissions form
利润及提成险

profit-sharing plan
利润分享计划

profit squeeze
套取利润，利润压缩

profit system
利润制度

profit taking
获利回吐，套购谋利

program budgeting
方案预算编制

programmer
编程员

programming language (c)
编程语言

program trade
集团股票交易

progressive tax
累进税

progress payments
施工分期付款，按进度付款

projected benefit obligation
预期福利责任

projected (pro forma) financial statement
预期（预计）财务报表

projection
预测

promissory note
本票，期票，借据

promotional allowance
推销津贴，促销津贴

promotion mix
推广组合，促销组合

proof of loss
损失证明

property
财产，地产

property line
地产边界线

property management
财产管理

property report
财产报告

property rights
财产权，产权

property tax
财产税

proprietary interest
专利，业主权益

proprietary lease
产权租赁

proprietorship
独资企业，资本净值，所有制

prorate
按比例分配

prospect
潜在的顾客，前景

prospective rating
预期评级

prospectus
说明书，计划书

protected file (c)
保护文件

protectionism
保护主义

protocol
协议书，协定草案

proviso
但书，限制性条款

proxy
代理人，代表，委托书，授权书

proxy fight
委托书争夺

proxy statement
委托书

prudence
慎重，谨慎

psychic income
心理收入，精神收益

public accounting
公众会计，公共会计

public domain
公有财产

public employee
公务员

public file (c)
公共文件

publicly held
公众持股公司

public record
土地公开记录，法庭公开记录

public relations (PR)
公共关系（PR）

public sale
公卖，拍卖，专卖

public use
公共使用

public works
公共项目

puffing
哄抬

pull-down menu (c)
下拉式选单

pump priming
刺激经济政策

punch list
修正项目

punitive damages
惩罚性损害赔偿

purchase
买，购买，采购，
议付

purchase journal
采购分录账

**purchase money
mortgage**
购买财产担保

purchase order
购货定单，
定货单

purchasing power
购买力

pure capitalism
纯资本主义

pure competition
纯粹竞争，完全竞争

**pure-market
economy**
完全市场经济

purge (c)
清除

push money (PM)
推销奖金

put option
卖期货的权利，出售选择权

put to seller
卖方出售权

pyramiding
金字塔式控制股权

p **value**
p 值

Q

qualified endorsement
附条件背书，限制背书

qualified opinion
限定意见，保留意见

qualified plan or qualified trust
附条件老年金计划或附条件信托

qualified terminable interest property (Q-TIP) trust
附条件可终止利息财产（Q-TIP）信托

qualitative analysis
定性分析

qualitative research
定性研究

quality
质量，品质，优质的，高级的

quality control
质量管理，品质控制

quality engineering
质量工程

quantitative analysis
定量分析

quantitative research
定量研究

quantity discount
数量折扣

quarterly
季度的

quasi contract
准契约，准合同

query (c)
查询；询问程序

queue (c)
队列，排队

quick asset
速动资产，可兑现资产

quick ratio
速动比率，偿付力比率

quiet enjoyment
安静享受权

quiet title suit
不活跃产权诉讼

quitclaim deed
放弃权利契约

quorum
必须到法庭的法定人数

quota
配额，限额，指标

quota sample
定额样本

quotation
报价，行情，估价表

quo warranto
责问某人根据什么行使职权的令状

qwerty keyboard (c)
qwerty 键盘

R

racket
诈骗，敲诈
rag content
纸中棉花纤维含量百分比
raider
袭击者，
市场扰乱者
rain insurance
雨淋险
raised check
涂改金额的支票，
伪造支票
rally
回升
random access
memory
(RAM) (c)
随机存取存储器
(RAM）
random-digit
dialing
随机拨号选择
random-number
generator
随机号码发生器
random
sample
随机样本
random walk
随机运动

range
全距，范围，规模，
(c) 范围，值域，
量程
rank-and file
一般付费工会成员
ratable
可估价的
rate
率，比例，价格，
费用，定额，行情
rate base
运价率基数，
收费标准
rate card
价目牌
rated policy
标准保单
rates and
classifications
费率及分类
rate setting
劳动定额，
工资定额
ratification
批准，通过
rating
评价，
评级

ratio analysis
比率分析

rationing
配额

ratio scale
比率尺度，等比量表

raw data
原始数据

raw land
生地，未开发土地

raw material
原料

reading the
tape
监视股票价格涨落

readjustment
再调整

read-only (c)
只读

real
真实的，实际的

real account
真实账户，实账

real earnings
实际收益

real estate
房地产，不动产

real estate investment trust
(REIT)
房地产投资信托
（REIT）

real estate market
房地产市场

real estate owned
(REO)
备用房地产（REO）

real income
实际收入

real interest rate
实际利率

realized gain
实现收益

real property
不动产，房地产

real rate of return
实际回报率

realtor
房地产经纪人

real value of money
实际货币价值

real wages
实际工资

reappraisal lease
重估租赁

reasonable person
通情达理之人

reassessment
更正

rebate
回扣，折扣，退税

reboot (c)
再引导，
重新启动

recall
收回，(c) 复检，
二次呼叫

recall campaign
产品收回广告

recall study
产品收回研究

recapitalization
资本重组

recapture
回收，收复，归公

recapture rate
回收率

recasting a debt
债务重新安排

receipt, receipt book
收据，收款凭单簿

receivables turnover
应收款周转率

receiver
清算人，收款人

receiver's certificate
清算人借款证

receivership
财力清算，
清算管理

receiving clerk
收货员，收料员，
验收员

receiving record
收货记录

recession
经济衰退

reciprocal buying
相互购买

reciprocity
互惠，交换

reckoning
计算，估算

recognition
确认

recognized gain
公认收益

recompense
偿还，补偿，赔偿

reconciliation
调节，调停，调和

reconditioning property
维修财产

reconsign
再委托，再托卖

reconveyance
再转让

record
记录，记载项目

recorder point
记录点

recording
入账，记录

records management
账目管理

recoup, recoupment
补偿，赔偿，扣除

recourse
索赔，追索

recourse loan
索赔贷款，
偿还贷款

recover (c)
恢复

recovery
追索，追赔，收回，
恢复

recovery fund
追偿基金

recovery of basis
基本成本收回

recruitment
招聘，征收

recruitment bonus
招聘奖金

recycle bin (c)
回收站

recycling
回收，再循环

redeem
赎回，偿还，履行，兑现

redemption
赎买，抵消，弥补，偿还

redemption period
赎回期，偿还期

redevelop
再开发

rediscount
现贴现，转贴现

rediscount rate
再贴现率

redlining
基于种族原因的贷款限制

red tape
红章，官僚主义

reduced rate
降低费率

reduction certificate
贷款余额证明

referee
仲裁人，公断人，鉴定人

referral
转介

refinance
再筹措资金

reformation
改革，改良，改善，调整

refresh (c)
刷新；重新整理

refunding
再融资，举债还债，发行新债券取代旧债券

refund
偿还，退款

registered bond
登记债券，记名债券

registered check
记名支票

registered company
法人公司，注册公司

registered investment company
注册投资公司

registered representative
登记代表

registered security
记名债券

registrar
注册官，登记股票转让的信托公司

registration
注册，登记，挂号

registration statement
注册上市申请书

registry of deeds
契约登记处

regression analysis
回归分析

regression line
回归线

regressive tax
递减税

regular-way delivery
(and settlement)
正常交货（常规结算）

regulated commodities
管制商品

regulated industry
管制工业

regulated investment
company
管制投资公司

regulation
规章，条例，管理，
控制，调整

regulatory agency
管理机构

rehabilitation
修复，恢复

reindustrialization
再工业化

reinstatement
续保，复职，复原，
恢复权利

reinsurance
再保险，分保

reinvestment
privilege
再投资特权

reinvestment rate
再投资率

related party

transaction
集团内交易

release
解除，免除，卸货，放行，
放弃，宣布

release clause
解除条款

relevance
相关

reliability
可信性，可靠性

relocate
重新安置

remainder
剩余财产

remainderman
剩余财产受益人

remedy
补救，赔偿，贴水

remit
汇款，免除，提交，移交

remit rate
免除率

remonetization
再货币化

remote access (c)
远程存取，远程访问

remuneration
薪酬，报酬，补偿

renegotiate
再谈判，重新协商

renegotiated rate mortgage
(RRM)
利率重订抵押贷款（RRM）

renewable natural resource
可再生自然能源

renewal option
可续期选择权

rent
租，租金，房租，承租，
期款

rentable area
可租赁面积

rental rate
租率

rent control
租金控制

rent-free period
租金免付期

rent-up period
租金上涨期

reopener clause
重开谈判条款

reorganization
改组

repairs
修理，修补，修缮

repatriation
收回，返回

replace (c)
替换，代换，置换

replacement cost
重置费用，重置成本

replacement cost
accounting
重置成本会计

replacement reserve
重置储备金

replevin
没收物的发还

reporting currency
申报货币

repressive tax
抑制性税收

reproduction cost
复制成本，再生产成本

repudiation
拒绝，废弃，拒付

repurchase agreement
(REPO; RP)
证券重购买协议，
购回协定（REPO；RP）

reputation
信誉，声望

request for proposal
(RFP)
征询报价，征询方案

required rate of return
应得报酬率

requisition
申请书，请款单，
领料单

resale proceeds
重售收入

rescission
解约，撤销，废除，
解除

research
研究，分析，考察，
调查

research and
development (R&D)
研究和发展，研制
（R&D））

research department
研究部门

research intensive
研究密集型

reserve
储备，准备金，保存
reserve fund
储备基金，后备基金
reserve requirement
准备金规定，
储备要求
reserve-stock control
库存储备控制
reset (c)
复位
resident buyer
常驻采购员
resident buying
office
常驻采购办公室
residential
住宅
residential broker
住宅地产经纪人
residential district
住宅区
residential energy credit
住宅能源信贷
residential service
contract
住宅服务合同
residual value
余值，残值，
剩余成本
resolution
决心，果断，决议，
解决
resource
资源，物资，财力，
资产

respondent
答辩者，被告
response
回应，反应
response projection
反应预测
restitution
退回，归还，赔偿，
恢复
restraint of trade
贸易限制
restraint on
alienation
转让限制
restart (c)
重新启动，再启动
restricted surplus
限制性盈余
restriction
限制，限定，约束，
管制
restrictive covenant
限制贸易契约
retail
零售，零售的
retail credit
零售信用
retail display
allowance
零售商品展示回扣
retailer's service
program
零售商服务项目
retail inventory
method
零售价盘存法

retail outlet
零售销路

retail rate
零售商广告费率

retaining
保留，保持

retained earnings
保留盈余，
留存收益

retained earnings appropriated
已分配留存收益

retained earnings statement
留存收益表

retaliatory eviction
报复性驱逐

retire
兑清票据，赎票，付清，
退休

retirement
赎票，退休金，
退股，偿还

retirement age
退休年龄

reitrement fund
退休基金

retirement income
退休收入

retirement plan
退休计划

retroactive
追溯，追加

retroactive adjustment
追溯调整

return
退货，报酬，收益，
赢利

return of capital
资本收益率

return on equity
权益报酬率

return on invested capital
投入资本收益率，
投资报酬率

return on pension plan assets
老年金计划资产回报率

return on sales
销售利润率

returns
退货，报酬，
收益

revaluation
重估价值，再评价

revenue
收入，收益

revenue anticipation note (RAN)
收入预期票据（RAN）

revenue bond
收益债券

revenue ruling
收入裁决

reversal
反向

reverse annuity mortgage (RAM)
反向年金抵押
（RAM）

reverse leverage
反向影响

reverse split
并股

reversing entry
反向分录，
转回分录

reversion
回复，修正

reversionary factor
反向因子

reversionary interest
可享有的利益

reversionary value
应继承的价值

review
再检查，分析考察，
审查

revocable trust
可取消信托

revocation
取消，废除，撤回，
撤销

revolving charge account
循环费用账户

revolving credit
周转信贷

revolving fund
周转基金

rezoning
重新分区

rich
价格太高的证券，
太高的利率，富有

rich text format (RTF) (c)
多信息文本格式
（RTF）

rider
批单，追加条款，
附则

right of first refusal
优先购买权

right of redemption
赎买权，买回权

right of rescission
解约权，撤销权

right of return
退货权

right of survivorship
承继权

right-of-way
过境权，地段权

risk
危险，风险，保险种类，
保险

risk-adjusted discount rate
按风险调整贴现率

risk arbitrage
风险套利

risk averse
不愿承担风险，风险反感

risk management
风险管理

rolling stock
轮式运输设备

rollover
以新债券代替旧债券，
纳税递延交易

rollover loan
展期贷款，
循环贷款

ROM (read-only memory) (c)
ROM（只读存储器）

rotating shift
轮班

roundhouse
圆形机车库

round lot
整数批量，整份

royalty
专利税，版权税

royalty trust
特许权信托

run
有效，运货，循环，流动，
连续，经营

rundown
逐项核对

run of paper (ROP)
报纸广告位置（ROP）

run with the land
对土地所有人产生影响的权
利或限制

rural
农村的

rurban
郊外住宅区的

service
服务，业务，公共事业，
公营机构，检修

service bureau
服务机构

service club
服务性社团

service
department
服务部门

service economy
服务经济

service fee
服务费

service worker
服务人员

servicing
日常维修，贷款服务

setback
挫折，倒退

setoff
抵消

settle
解决，结算，偿付，
定居

settlement
决算，结算，解决，
处理

settlement date
决算日期

settlor
财产授与人

severalty
土地的个人拥有权

severance damages
分割损害

severance pay
解雇金，遣散费

sexual harassment
性骚扰

shakedown
试航，试验

shakeout
股票市场的暴跌，
景气的消退

shakeup
[公司机构等的]大改革，
大变动

share
股，股份，股票，股权，
份额，分配

sharecropper
小佃农

shared-appreciation
mortgage (SAM)
分成增值抵押
（SAM）

shared drive (c)
共享驱动器

shared-equity
mortgage
分成股本抵押

shareholder
股东，股票持有人

shareholder's
equity
股东权益

shares authorized
核准股票

shareware (c)
共享软件，
共用软件

shark repellent
防止被收购的拒鲨行动
shark watcher
监视收购活动的公司
sheet feeder (c)
供[送]纸器
shell corporation
空壳公司
shift
转让，转移，改变，
替换，换班
shift differential
班次补助，值班津贴
shift key (c)
换档键
shift lock (c)
换档锁
shop
商店，车间，工厂
shopper
买东西的顾客，
购物人
shopping service
采购服务
short bond
短期债券
short covering
抛空补回，空头补进
shortfall
不足，亏空
short form
简式
short interest
空头净额
short position
空头

short-sale rule
卖空规则
short squeeze
空头轧平，杀空头
short term
短期
**short-term capital
gain (loss)**
短期资本收益
（损失）
**short-term debt or
short-term liability**
短期债务或短期负债
shrinkage
价值下降，收缩，
损耗
shut down (c)
关机
shutdown
停业，停工
sight draft
即期汇票
sign off (c)
结束指令
sign on (c)
开始指令
silent partner
隐名合伙人
silver standard
银本位
**SIMM (single in-line
memory module) (c)**
SIMM
（单列直插式内存模块）
simple interest
单利

simple trust
简单信托，单纯信托

simple yield
简单收益

simulation
模拟，模仿，仿真，
伪装

single-entry bookkeeping
单式簿记

single premium life insurance
一次性付清保费的人寿保险

sinking fund
累积基金，偿债基金

site
地点，现场，位置，
工地

site audit
就地审计

sit-down strike
围厂停产罢工

skill intensive
技术密集型

skill obsolescence
过时的技能

slack
萧条期，淡季，
松弛的

slander
诽谤，诋毁

sleeper
爆冷门的股票

sleeping beauty
潜在收购目标

slowdown
需求下降，放慢

slump
价格狂跌，市场萧条

small business
小型企业

small investor
小型投资者

smoke clause
烟雾险条款

smokestack industry
冒烟工业，重工业

snowballing
滚雪球式业务增长

social insurance
社会保险

socialism
社会主义

socially conscious investor
有社会责任感的投资者

social responsibility
社会责任

soft currecy
软币，软性货币

soft goods
纺织品，软货物，
非耐用品

soft market
疲软的市场

soft money
软币，汇票

soft spot
不景气企业

soil bank
土地银行

sole proprietorship
独资企业，独资经营

solvency
偿付能力，
支付能力

source
根据，来源，出处，
销售渠道

source evaluation
销售渠道评估

sources of funds
资金来源

source worksheet (c)
源工作底稿，源表

sovereign risk
政治风险，政府风险，
主权国风险

space bar (c)
空格键

spamming (c)
滥言

span of control
管理幅度

special agent
特别助理，
特别调查员

special assignment
特别任务

special delivery
专递

special drawing rights
(SDR)
特别提款权
（SDR）

special handling
特别处理服务

specialist
专家，交易所经纪人

special purchase
专项采购

special situation
特殊情况

specialty advertising
特色宣传广告

specialty goods
特色物品，特殊商品

specialty retailer
特色商品零售商

specialty selling
特色商品销售

specialty shop
特色商店

special-use permit
专用许可证

special warranty
deed
特别保证契约

specie
铸币，硬币，现金

specification
规格，说明，技术要求

specific identification
个别鉴定法

specific performance
个别行为

specific subsidy
个别补贴

speculative risk
投机风险

speech
recognition (c)
语音识别

speedup
加速

spell checker (c)
拼写检查程序

spending money
零用钱，花费

spendthrift trust
规定受益人不得自由处理
的信托资产

spider chart (c)
蛛网图

spillover
溢出，溢出物

spin-off
母公司收回子公司全部股
本使之脱离的作法，让产
易股，折产为投

splintered authority
意见纷纭的管理机关

split
分割，分摊，分股

split commission
佣金平分

split shift
间断工时

spokesperson
发言人

sponsor
保证人，担保人，主持人，
主办人

spot check
抽样，抽查，现场检查

spot commodity
现货，现货商品

spot delivery month
当场交货月份

spot market
现货交易市场

spot price
现货价格

spot zoning
现场土地重划

spread
分录过账，赢利，差幅，
跨栏目广告

spreading agreement
分散担保协议

spread sheet
电子表格

squatter's rights
斯夸特权利

squeeze
压榨，挤兑，剥削，回扣，
使缩减，买回

stabilization
稳定，稳定作用，
安全

stacked column chart (c)
堆积柱形图

staggered election
交错选举

staggering maturities
证券交错到期

stagnation
停滞，萧条，不景气

stake
投机股本

stand-alone system
独立系统

standard
标准，规则，定额，
本位

standard cost
标准成本

standard deduction
标准扣除额

standard deviation
标准偏差

standard industrial
classification (SIC)
system
标准产业分类 （SIC）
系统

standard of living
生活水准

standard time
标准时间

standard wage rate
标准工资率

standby fee
候补押金

standby (c)
备用，辅助

standby loan
备用贷款

standing order
标准定单

staple stock
大路货，大宗货物

start-up
新创企业

start-up screen (c)
启动屏幕

stated value
设定价值

statement
账单，报表，财务报告，
清账，陈述

statement of affairs
业务报告,
财产状况说明书

statement of
condition
状况表,
借贷对照表

statement of partners'
capital
合伙人资金报表

static anaylsis
静态分析

static budget
静态预算

static risk
固定风险

statistic
统计的，统计学的

statistical inference
统计性推论

statistically significant
有统计学意义的

statistical sampling
统计抽样

statistics
统计，统计学

status
效力，情况，地位，
资格

status bar (c)
状态栏

status symbol
地位标志

statute
章程，法规，
条例

statute of frauds
反欺骗法
statute of limitations
法定追索期限，
诉讼时效法
statutory audit
法定审计
statutory merger
法定合并
statutory notice
法定通知
statutory voting
法定投票
staying power
持久力，耐久性
steady-growth
method
均衡增长法
steering
非法限制某一族裔团体获
得住房
stepped-up basis
税基上调
stipend, stipendiary
薪水，定期生活津贴
stipulation
规定，条款，条件
stochastic
随机的
stock
股份，股票，证券，
库存，存料
stockbroker
股票经纪人
stock certificate
股票，股权证

stock dividend
股息，股利
stock exchange
股票交易所，
证券交易
stockholder
股东
stockholder of record
注册股东
stockholder's derivative
action
股东派生诉讼
stockholder's equity
股东股本
stock index future
股票指数期货
stock insurance
company
股票保险公司
stock jobbing
证券批发
stock ledger
股东名册，
存货分类账
stock market
股市，证券市场
stock option
认股权，股票购买权
stockout cost
缺货成本
stockpile
储存，囤储
stock power
股票转让授权书
stock record
股票记录

stockroom
商品陈列室，
商品储藏室

stock symbol
股票代号

stock turnover
存货周转率，
证券交易额

stonewalling
拒绝承认，拒绝合作

stool pigeon
间谍，线人

stop clause
终止合同条款

stop-loss reinsurance
停止损失再保险

stop order
预定低点抛售，限额定单，
中止命令

stop payment
止付，停付

store
货仓，储存，商店

store brand
商店自名产品

straddle
限价套利，
股票买卖选择权

straight bill of lading
直接提单，记名提单

straight-line method of depreciation
直线折旧法，
平均折旧法

straight-line production
直线生产

straight time
单纯记时

straphanger
拉着吊环站立的乘客，
乘车上下班的人

strategic planning
战略规划

strategy
战略，策略

stratified random sampling
分层随机抽样

straw boss
临时领导

straw man
稻草人，假想敌，
身无分文的人

street name
记在经纪人名下的客户证券

stretchout
无偿加班，展期

strike
定价，定约，
罢工

strike benefits
罢工期间福利

strikebreaker
罢工期间由管理层雇用的
人手

strike notice
罢工通知

strike pay
罢工工资

strike price
成交价格

strike vote
罢工投票

strip
债券分开出售

structural inflation
结构性通货膨胀

structural
unemployment
结构性失业

structure
结构，体制，构成，
构造

subcontractor
分包商

subdirectory (c)
子目录

subdivider
土地分块出售者

subdividing
土地分块

subdivision
用于建房的地块

subject to
mortgage
尚待抵押贷款

sublease
转租

sublet
转租，分租

subliminal
advertising
潜性广告

submarginal
低于边际的

suboptimize
未发挥最大潜力

subordinated
次等的，附属的

subordinate debt
次要债务

subordination
次要，附属，从属

subpoena
传票

subrogation
代位求偿权，
权益转让

subroutine
子程序

subscript
下标，(c) 下标，
脚注

subscripted
variable
带下标的变量

subscription
认股，定购，签署，
订阅

subscription price
订价，认定价

subscription
privilege
认股优先权

subscription
right
认股权

subsequent event
后发事件，
结账后发生的事项

subsidiary
附属公司，子公司，
分行，辅助的

subsidiary company
附属公司，子公司

subsidiary ledger
明细分类账
subsidy
补助金，津贴，
奖励金
subsistence
维持生活
substitution
代替，取代，替换，
代位
substitution effect
替代效应
substitution law
替代法则
substitution slope
替代斜率
subtenant
转租人，次承租人
subtotal
合计
suggested retail price
建议零售价
suggestion system
职工建议系统
suicide clause
人寿保险中的自杀条款
suite (c)
套；(程序)组
summons
传讯，传票
sunset industry
夕阳工业
sunset provision
法律或法规有效期条款

superfund
联邦政府设立用于清理危
险性污染的基金
superintendent
总督，总监
supermarket
超级市场
super now account
存款额越高利息越高的一
种银行账户
supersaver fare
超储费
superscript (c)
上标
super sinker bond
超跌价债券
superstore
超级市场，超级商店
supplemental agreement
补充协议
supplier
供应商，供货人
supply
供应，提供
supply price
供货价
supply-side economics
供应经济学派
support level
支持价
surcharge
超载，额外费用，
附加税
surety bond
担保债券，
担保书

surge protector (c)
浪涌保护器

surplus
盈余，剩余物资，
贸易顺差

surrender
交出，提交，放弃，
缴纳，退保

surrender, life insurance
人寿保险退保

surtax
附加税

survey
勘查，鉴定，检验，
评论

survey area
勘查地区

surveyor
鉴定师，公证人，
海关验货员

survivorship
生存

suspended trading
中断贸易

suspense account
暂记账，悬账

suspension
停止支付，中止，
暂停营业

swap
掉换，交换，互惠信贷

sweat equity
通过改进使财产增值

sweatshop
血汗工厂

sweepstakes
彩票

sweetener
证券附加特点

swing shift
小夜班[下午 4-12 时的值班]

switching
转手

symbol bar (c)
符号栏

sympathetic strike
同情性罢工

syndicate
辛迪加，企业组合垄断，
财团

syndication
辛迪加组织

syndicator
财团投资人

synergy
协同，
企业合并后的协力优势

system
系统，制度，体系，
(c) 系统，体制

system administrator (c)
系统管理员

systematic risk
无法避免的风险

systematic sampling
系统性抽样

T

T-account
T 形账户

tab key (c)
制表键

table column (c)
表格列

table field (c)
表栏，表域

tactic
战术

tag sale
自家旧货售卖

take a bath, take a beating
投资失败，
遭受巨大损失

take a flier
冒险行事，投机

take a position
购买股票

take-home pay
净剩工资

take
拿，取，获得

takeoff
起飞，稳定

take-out loan, take-out financing
取代贷款，
取代融资

takeover
收购，合并

taking
取得土地

taking delivery
接收货物

taking inventory
盘存，盘货

tally
点数，理货，记账，
标签

tangible asset
有形资产，
实际资产

tangible personal property
有形个人财产

tank car
油罐车

tape
磁带，胶带，
录音带

target audience
目标听众

target file (c)
目标文件

target group index (TGI)
目标群组指数
（TGI）

- 148 -

target market
目标市场

target price
目标价格，标准价格

tariff
关税率，运费率，票价

tariff war
关税战

task bar (c)
任务条[栏]

task force
工作组

task group
任务小组

task list (c)
任务列表

task manager (c)
任务管理器

task management
任务管理

tax
税，税款，支付，评定

tax abatement
减税

taxable income
应税收入

taxable year
应税年度

tax and loan account
税收与借款账户

tax anticipation bill (TAB)
先期交税债券（TAB）

tax anticipation note (TAN)
税收预期票据（TAN）

taxation, interest on dividends
股息税

tax base
计税基础

tax bracket
税收等级

tax credit
税收抵免

tax deductible
免税，税务扣减

tax deduction
税额扣减，免税，减税

tax deed
税务契据

tax deferred
递延税务

tax evasion
逃税，偷税

tax-exempt property
免税财产

tax-exempt security
免税证券

tax foreclosure
因未交税而取消赎回权的没收财产

tax-free exchange
免税资产交换

tax impact
税赋影响

tax incentive
税收鼓励

tax incidence
课税归宿，纳税负担

tax lien
课税扣押权

tax loss carryback
(carryforward)
赋税亏损转回
（结转）

tax map
土地税务图

taxpayer
纳税人

tax planning
计划避税

tax preference item
优惠税率项目

tax rate
税率

tax return
税单，纳税申报表

tax roll
税率，税款清册

tax sale
欠税财产的拍卖

tax selling
纳税抛售

tax shelter
避税办法

tax stop
纳税停止线

tax straddle
税收套购

tax wedge
税务原因

team building
团队建设

team management
团队管理

teaser ad
含蓄而令人好奇的广告

teaser rate
最初利率

technical analysis
技术分析

technical rally
技术性回升

technological
obsolescence
技术陈旧

technological
unemployment
技术性失业

technology
技术，工艺，术语

telecommunications
电讯

telemarketing
电话营销

telephone switching
通过电话转移互助基金资产

template
模板

tenancy
租赁，租期，租借权

tenancy at
sufferance
过期租赁

tenancy at will
意愿性租赁

tenancy by the
entirety
整体租赁

tenancy for years
固定期限租赁

tenancy in common
共同租赁

tenancy in severalty
单独租赁

tenant
承租人，租户，房客，
租借

tenant finish-out allowance
租户整改折扣

tender
投标，清偿，提出，
投标书

tender of delivery
提供运送服务

tender offer
收购股权，招标，
提出要约

tenure
占用，占有，使用期

tenure in land
土地占有

term
期限，条款，约定，
术语，结账期

term, amortization
摊还期

term certificate
定期存款证明

termination benefits
解雇福利

term life insurance
定期人手保险

term loan
定期贷款

terms
条款

test
检验，测试，
测验方法

testament
遗嘱

testamentary trust
遗嘱信托

testate
有遗嘱的

testator
立有遗嘱的人

testcheck
抽查，抽查法

testimonial
奖金，纪念品，证明书，
鉴定书

testimonium
援引条款

test market
试销市场

test statistic
调查统计

text editing (c)
正文[文本]编辑

text processing (c)
正文[文本]处理

text wrap (c)
正文[文本]围绕

thin market
滞呆市场，
清淡市场

third market
第三市场
third party
第三方，第三者
third-party check
第三者支票
third-party sale
第三者销售
threshold-point
ordering
起点订购
thrift insitution
储蓄机构
thrifty
廉价的
through rate
联运运费，直达运价
tick
信用，赊欠，赊销，
赊购
ticker
股票行情自动收录器
tie-in promotion
联合推销
tight market
供不应求的市场
tight money
收紧银根
tight ship
严格的规章制度
till
备用现金，钱柜
time-and-a-half
一点五倍加班费
time card
工时卡

time deposit
定期存款
time draft
定期汇票，远期汇票
time is of the essence
强调时间要素的重要性，
时限
time management
时间管理
time series
analysis
时序分析
time series data
时序数据
time-sharing
分时
timetable
时间表，时刻表
time value
时间价值
tip
小费，内幕消息，
暗示，劝告
title
产权，权利，所有权，
科目，名称
title bar (c)
标题栏[条]
title company
产权调查公司
title defect
产权缺陷
title insurance
产权保险
title report
产权报告

- 152 -

title screen (c)
标题屏幕

title search
产权搜索

title theory
产权理论

toggle key (c)
切换键

tokenism
象征主义

toll
通行税，过境税，
长途电话费，服务费

tombstone ad
证券发行广告

toner cartridge (c)
墨粉盒

tool bar (c)
工具栏

tool box (c)
工具箱

topping out
市场或证券达到顶点

tort
侵权

total capitalization
总资本结构

total loss
总亏损，亏损总额，
全损险

total paid
总付款

total volume
总额，总量

touch screen (c)
触摸屏

trace, tracer
追踪，追询书

trackage
铁路轨道使用费

trackball (c)
跟踪球

tract
一片土地

trade
贸易，商业，交易，
买卖，行业

trade acceptance
商业承兑汇票

trade advertising
消费品广告

trade agreement
贸易协议

trade barrier
贸易壁垒

trade credit
贸易赊账，商业信用

trade date
交易日期，成交日期

trade deficit (surplus)
贸易赤字（盈余）

trade fixture
工商业设备，
贸易设施

trade magazine
贸易杂志

trademark
商标

trade-off
卖掉，换掉

trade rate
同业汇率

trader
贸易商，交易员，
商船

trade secret
商业秘密，行业秘密

trade show
商业展览

trade union
工会，行业工会

trading
authorization
贸易委托书

trading post
交易所，商站

trading range
成交价格幅度

trading stamp
购货赠券，
商品券

trading unit
交易单位

traditional economy
传统经济

tramp
不定期货船

transaction
交易，业务，
会计事项

transaction cost
交易费用，
交易成本

transfer agent
过户代理人

transfer development
rights
转让开发权

transfer payment
转账性支付，
转付款项

transfer price
转让价

transfer tax
转让税

translate
翻译，折算，
换算

transmit a virus (c)
传输病毒

transmittal letter
转让信

transnational
跨国的

transportation
运输，运输业，
货运，交通

treason
叛逆，背信弃义

treasurer
司库，财务主任，
出纳员

tree diagram
树形图

trend
趋势，倾向，动向

trend chart (c)
趋势图

trend line
经济趋势线

trespass
非法侵入，非法侵害

trial and error
检误，反复性试验

trial balance
试算法，总账平衡法

trial offer
试发盘

trial subscriber
试用用户

trigger point
触发点

trigger price
触发价格，基准价格

triple-net lease
净租赁

Trojan Horse (c)
特洛伊木马，欺骗软件，
欺骗程序

troubled debt restructuring
滞还债款重整

troubleshooter
发现和解决问题的人

troubleshooting (c)
故障寻找

trough
衰退谷底

true lease
正式租约

true to scale (c)
标度正确的

truncation
切断，剪断

trust
信托，委托，联合垄断，
信用

trust account
信托账户，托管财产

trust certificate
委托证书，信托证券

trust company
信托公司

trust deed
信托契约，委托书

trust, discretionary
任意决定信托

trustee
托管人，受托人

trustee in bankruptcy
破产管理人

trust fund
信托基金

trust, general
management
普通管理信托

trustor
信托人，
财产授予者

truth in lending act
贷款真实法案

turkey
失败的投资

turnaround
周转

turnaround time
周转时间

turnkey
统包方式，
'交钥匙'方式

turn off (c)
断开，关断

turn on (c)
接通，开启

turnover
营业额，周转额，
销售额

twisting
翘曲，扭曲

two-tailed test
双边假设性检验

two percent rule
百分之二规则

***T* statistic**
T 统计

tycoon
工商巨头，大亨

typeface (c)
字样

type-over mode (c)
改写模式

U

umbrella liability
insurance
总括责任险
unappropriated retained
earnings
未分配保留收益
unbalanced growth
不平衡增长
unbiased estimator
无偏估计
uncollected funds
未结清资金
uncollectible
无法兑付的，
无法收取的
unconsolidated
subsidiary
不合并计算的子公司
underapplied
overhead
少分配的制造费用
undercapaliztion
资本不足，投资不足
underclass
社会地层
underemployed
高能低就
underground
economy
地下经济

underinsured
保险不足
underline (c)
下划线
underlying debt
第一债务
underlying mortgage
第一担保抵押
underlying security
抵押担保
underpay
支付不足
under the counter
私下交易，贿赂
undervalued
估值偏低
underwriter
保险商，包销商，
承销人
underwriting
spread
承保差额
undiscounted
未打折扣
undivided
interest
不可分割的利益
undivided
profit
未分利润

undue influence
不当影响

unearned discount
未获折扣，未得贴现

unearned income (revenue)
非营业收入（收益）

unearned increment
自然增值

unearned interest
已收到但未实现的利息

unearned premium
未满期保险费

unemployable
无法就业的

unemployed labor force
失业劳动力

unemployment
失业，未就业，无工作

unencumbered property
未支配财产，
未承担债务财产

unexpired cost
未抵消成本，
未耗成本

unfair competition
不公平竞争

unfavorable balance of trade
贸易逆差

unfreeze
解除限制

unified estate and gift tax
统一遗产税和赠与税

unilateral contract
单边契约

unimproved property
未作改进的财产

unincorporated association
未注册协会

unique impairment
独特损害

unissued stock
未发行股票

unit
单位，单元

unitary elasticity
单一弹性

unit-labor cost
单位劳动成本

unit of trading
成交单位

units-of-production method
生产单位折旧法

unity of command
统一指挥

universal life insurance
综合人寿保险

universal product code (UPC)
通用商品代码
（UPC）

unlisted security
非挂牌证券

unloading
卸货，抛售，倾销，
支持

unoccupancy
空置

unpaid dividend
未付利息

unrealized profit (loss)
未实现利润
（损失）

unrecorded deed
未列契据

unrecoverable (c)
不可恢复的

unrecovered cost
未收回成本

unsecured debt
无担保债务

unskilled
不熟练的

unwind a trade
反向交易

update
更新
(c) 更改，更新

up front
即付现金，
坦率的

upgrade (c)
升级，更新

upgrade software (c)
升级软件

upgrading
提高，改进，提高等级

upkeep
保养，维修，管理

upload (c)
上载

upper case letter (c)
大写字母

upright format (c)
垂直格式

upside potential
股票的可能上涨幅度

upswing
好转，增加

up tick
交易价上涨，
股票报升

uptrend
上升趋势

upwardly mobile
上移阶层

urban
城市的，都市的

urban renewal
城市再开发

useful life
有用年限，可用寿命

user (c)
用户

user authorization (c)
用户特许文件

user manual (c)
用户手册

usufructuary right
用益权，使用权

usury
高利贷

utility
共用事业，共用设施，
效用

utility easement
共用设施的地役权

utility program (c)

实用程序

V

vacancy rate
闲置率，空房率
vacant
空置，空闲
vacant land
土地闲置
vacate
取消，辞职
valid
有效的，有根据的
valuable
consideration
有价值的对偿物
valuable papers (records)
insurance
有价证券（档案）
保险
valuation
估价，评价
value
价值，估价
value-added
tax
增值税
value date
起息日，交割日
value in exchange
交换价值
value line investment
survey
价值线投资调查

variable
变量
variable annuity
可变年金
variable cost
可变成本
variable interest rate
可变利率
variable life
insurance
变额人寿保险
variable pricing
差别定价
variable-rate mortgage
(VRM)
可变利率抵押贷款
variables sampling
变量采样
variance
差异，出入，
方差
variety store
杂货店
velocity
速度，周转率，流通速度
vendee
受货人，买方
vendor
卖主，商贩
vendor's lien
卖主留置权

venture
商业冒险，
短期投机
venture capital
投机资本
venture team
冒险小组
verbations
语言学上的词汇
vertical analysis
垂直分析，纵向分析
vertical discount
纵向时段广告折扣
vertical management structure
垂直管理结构
vertical promotion
垂直提升
vertical specialization
纵向专业化管理
vertical union
产业工会
vested interest
既得利益
vesting
授权
vicarious liability
转承责任，替代责任
vice-president
副总裁
video conference (c)
电视会议
video graphics board (c)
视频图形板
violation
违反，违背

virtual memory (c)
虚拟存储器
visual interface (c)
可视界面
vocational guidance
职业指南
vocational rehabilitation
恢复就业资格
voice mail (c)
语音邮件
voice recognition (c)
声音识别
voidable
可撤销的，可取消的
volatile
易变的，反复无常的
volume
体积，容积，
容量，数额
volume discount
大数量折扣
volume merchandise allowance
大额商品减价
voluntary accumulation plan
自愿购储计划
voluntary bankruptcy
自愿申请破产，自动倒闭
voluntary conveyance
无偿让与，自愿转让
voluntary lien
自愿留置权
voting right
投票权

voting stock

有投票权股

voting trust certificate

授权信托证书

voucher

传票，凭单，收据

voucher register

进货登记簿

W

wage
工资，工资基金，
雇佣
wage assignment
工资转让
wage bracket
工资等级
wage ceiling
最高工资限额
wage control
工资控制，
工资管理
wage floor
工资最低额
wage freeze
工资冻结
wage incentive
奖励工资
wage-push inflation
工资推动通货膨胀
wage rate
工资率，工资标准
wage scale
工资等级
wage stabilization
工资稳定化
waiver
放弃，免除，
弃权书

walkout
罢工，同盟罢工
wallflower
不受投资者青睐的股票
wallpaper (c)
壁[墙]纸
ware
商品，产品，货物
warehouse
仓库，货仓，货栈
warm boot/start (c)
热引导[启动]
warranty
保证书，保函，
保证条款
warranty deed
担保契约
warranty of
habitability
可居住保证
warranty of
merchantability
商品可销售性保证
wash sale
虚假交易，欺诈交易
waste
废料，浪费，滥用损耗
wasting asset
消耗资产，减耗资产

watch list
观察名单

watered stock
掺水股票，虚假

waybill
运货单，路程单

weakest link theory
最薄弱环节理论

weak market
疲软市场

wear and tear
损耗，磨损

wearout factor
失效因素

web browser (c)
万维网浏览器

web server (c)
万维网服务器

welfare state
福利国家

when issued
虚股交易，假若发行

whipsawed
遭受双重损失

white goods
大型家用电器，
白色货物

white knight
白衣骑士策略，
恶意收购解救人

white paper
白皮书

whole life insurance
终身人寿保险

whole loan
成套贷款

wholesaler
批发商

widget
小机械，装饰物

widow-and-orphan stock
高回报低风险的股票

wildcat drilling
不可靠的开采

wildcat strike
未经工会批准的罢工

will
遗嘱

windfall profit
意外利润，暴利

winding up
倒闭，停业，清理，
结束

windows application (c)
windows 应用程序

window
业务，橱窗，窗口
(c)窗口

window
dressing
窗帘，浮夸成果

wipeout
抹去，消除

wire house
联网经纪公司

withdrawal
提款，退股，撤销，
收回

withdrawal plan
提款计划

withholding
税款扣除

withholding tax
扣除税，预提税

without recourse
无追索权，
无偿还义务

wizard (c)
向导，范例

word processing (c)
文字处理

word wrapping (c)
字绕回，自动换行

work force
劳动力

working capital
运用资本，周转资金，
流动现金

work in progress
在制品，未完工程

workload
工作量，工作负荷

work order
工作单，任务单

workout
双方努力

work permit
工作许可证

worksheet
加工单，记工单
(c) 工作表，
工作单

work simplification
工作程序简化

work station
工作站

work stoppage
停工

work week
工作周

World Bank
世界银行

**world wide web
(www) (c)**
万维网

worm (c)
一种复制保护程序；
蠕虫

worth
资本，价值，财富

wraparound mortgage
环绕抵押贷款

wraparound type (c)
回绕类型

writ
令状，传票，法令，
文书

write error (c)
写入错误

write-protected (c)
写保护

writer
卖方，开票人，签署人

write-up
增记，增值，补写

writing naked
卖出非补进期权

writ of error
检误船票

written-down value
折旧后价值

XYZ

x-coordinate (c)
x-坐标
y-coordinate (c)
y-坐标
year-end
年终
year-end
dividend
年终股息
year-to-date
(YTD)
年初至当前日
（YTD）
yellow dog
contract
黄狗契约
yellow goods
非消耗性家居用品
yellow sheets
债券交易每日通报
yield
盈利，收益，盈利率，
产量
yield curve
收益率曲线
yield
equivalence
约当利率
yield
spread
收益率差价

yield to average
life
平均年限收益率
yield to call
至通知债券收益率
yield-to-mature
(YTM)
到期收益
（YTM）
yo-yo stock
"悠悠"股票
zero-base budgeting
(ZBB)
零基预算
（ZBB）
zero coupon bond
无息票债券
zero economic growth
经济无增长
zero lot line
零地界线
zero population growth
(ZPG)
人口无增长
（ZPG）
zero-sum game
零和游戏
zone of employment
工作区
zoning
分区

zoning map
区划图

zoning ordinance
市区划分法令

zoom function (c)
缩放功能

z score
Z 值

Order Form

Fax orders (Send this form): (301) 424-2518.
Telephone orders: Call 1(800) 822-3213 (in Maryland: (301)424-7737)
E-mail orders: spbooks@aol.com or: books@schreiberpublishing.com
Mail orders to:
Schreiber Publishing, 51 Monroe St., Suite 101, Rockville MD 20850 USA

Please send the following books, programs, and/or a free catalog. I under-
stand that I may return any of them for a full refund, for any reason, no
questions asked:
The Translator's Handbook 5th Revised Edition - $25.95
Spanish Business Dictionary - Multicultural Spanish - $24.95
German Business Dictionary - $24.95
French (France and Canada) Business Dictionary - $24.95
Chinese Business Dictionary - $24.95
Japanese Business Dictionary - $24.95
Russian Business Dictionary - $24.95
Global Business Dictionary (English, French, German, Chinese, Russian, Japanese) - $33.95
Spanish Chemical and Pharamceutical Glossary - $29.95
The Translator's Self-Training Program (circle the language/s of your
choice): Spanish French   German   Japanese Chinese   Italian
Portuguese   Russian   Arabic   Hebrew - $69.00
The Translator's Self-Training Program Spanish Medical   - $69.00
The Translator's Self-Training Program Spanish Legal - $69.00
The Translator's Self-Training Program - German Patents - $69.00
The Translator's Self-Training Program - Japanese Patents - $69.00
Multicultural Spanish Dictionary - How Spanish Differs from
Country to Country - $24.95
21st Century American English Compendium - The "Odds and Ends"
of American English Usage - $24.95
Dictionary of Medicine French/English - Over one million words of
medical terminology - $179.50
Name: _____

Address: _____

City: _____ State: _____ Zip: _____

Telephone: _____ e-mail: _____
Sales tax: Please add 5% sales tax in Maryland
Shipping (est.): $4 for the first book and $2.00 for each additional product
International: $ $9 for the first book, and $5 for each additional book
Payment: Cheque   Credit card: Visa   MasterCard

Card number: _____

Name on card: _____ Exp. Date: __/__